Women Powered!

Women Powered!

A New Paradigm
of Influence and Equity

THERESA DEL TUFO *and*
GEORGE BANEZ

Toplight

Jefferson, North Carolina

ISBN (print) 978-1-4766-8111-5
ISBN (ebook) 978-1-4766-4242-0

LIBRARY OF CONGRESS AND BRITISH LIBRARY
CATALOGUING DATA ARE AVAILABLE

Library of Congress Control Number 2021027464

Front cover: © 2021 PlusONE/Shutterstock

Printed in the United States of America

Toplight is an imprint of McFarland & Company, Inc., Publishers

*Box 611, Jefferson, North Carolina 28640
www.toplightbooks.com*

Table of Contents

Acknowledgments

I AM GRATEFUL TO MY PARENTS for instilling in me a passion for excellence and lifelong learning, and for serving as shining role models of how great leaders behave. Their words and actions showed me how to effectively and responsibly wield the temporal gift of power and influence. I feel blessed to have two good sons, who always believed in my abilities and made me feel valued—both as a woman and a leader—and supported my many creative and outlandish ventures. They always believed in me even when I failed to believe in myself. To Sam McKeeman, friend and mentor, for sharing his beautiful mind, kind heart, and inspiring spirit. Thank you for showing me and many others how to live life, with purpose and courage.

I stand on the shoulders of a pantheon of women—great women who came before me, great women who are walking hand-in-hand with me, and great women of the next decades who will continue the good fight for equality and parity. I am forever grateful for your courage, tenacity, resilience, and single-minded focus to overcome. Thank you to all the women and men who participated in our interviews and focus groups—who took time from their hectic schedules to share their astonishing experiences and their invaluable knowledge concerning this intractable and elusive social problem. My appreciation goes to Katie McDonough, who diligently and expertly edited my book, and to Christine Karpovage Rogers, for the descriptive and precise illustrations that made abstract concepts come alive. Katie's positive attitude, her authentic support, and her masterful editing skills inspired me to forge ahead despite the challenges. Finally, a Big "Thank-You!" to my colleague and friend, Dr. George Banez, for his

Acknowledgments

insightful portrayal of female leaders' experiences, triumphs, and challenges—all told with arresting detail and an uncommon flair. Thank you for sharing this journey of discovery and transformation with me.

Preface

I HAVE ALWAYS BEEN INTRIGUED why women are treated as second-class citizens in the United States of America, the greatest bastion of freedom and democracy in the world. I was born and raised in Asia, where women were traditionally subservient to men. But in the Philippines, I grew up feeling valued, respected, and equal in status to my brothers. There was no question that, like my brothers, I would enter college and have my own career, even if I should choose to get married. Even in the mid–1960s, women were doctors, engineers, architects, and governors, and they assumed positions of power in both government and business. When I immigrated to this country, I assumed leadership positions in different departments of the State of Delaware and noticed the absence of females in decision-making and leadership positions. Later, as an executive coach, I was baffled as to why women leaders appear to either *abdicate* or *abuse* power. This blatant role perversion confused and continues to confuse me. Why is there such a difficult and polarizing relationship between women and power?

The unexpected defeat of Hillary Clinton, a highly-experienced and trained professional woman, to an inexperienced businessman with no record of public service, was the final defining moment for me. It motivated me to rise above my anger and despair and do something to change the status quo. I am a lifelong learner, and I am passionate about concepts, ideas, and writing. The one significant move that I can make is to use my skills to write a book. I have dedicated the greater part of my life in this country to the improvement of the status of women in the areas of employment, education, training, and politics, so it seems fitting to capture my experience

1

and knowledge in a book—a fitting denouement to a lifetime of work.

It is my strong belief that our inability to gain and sustain power is due in large measure to our lack of knowledge of and experience in the exercise of power. In essence, **POWER** is the one critical component that is missing in our perilous journey toward equality and freedom. Although there have been significant steps toward gender parity, women still have major barriers to overcome to achieve a semblance of power and equality. In addition, it appears that progress has not followed a forward movement; it does not reflect a linear progression. The giant steps taken in the 1970s have not been sustained 50 years later. Despite major gains in 2018 in the political arena, the momentum for change inspired by the Me Too Movement and the narrowing of the wage gap and other notable achievements, American women are still far behind in their quest for equality (Warner, Ellmann, & Boesch, 2018).

Although there have been several books written on the subject of women and power, there has not been a publication that demonstrates in specific, systematic, and deliberate ways how to replicate the successes of women who have effectively wielded and kept power. What we need is a framework that captures the key *character and competency components* of effective women leaders who are able to wield power and influence and a *replicable process* to gain and sustain this elusive goal. Mary Beard's scholarly book *Women and Power: A Manifesto* (2017) is an historical monograph on the seeds of misogyny and an analysis of women's voices and roles since ancient times. Although she proposes a redefinition of power, which she claims is a male construct, she does not present an alternative framework that could serve as a guideline for action. *Women: Power and Prestige in Andean Society* (2017) by Moises Lemlij and Luis Millones is a "new interpretation on the role of women in Andean society, especially in the Moche culture and in the imperial Inca elite." Another publication, titled *The Power of Being a Woman: Secrets to Getting the Life You Want and the Love You Need,* is an account of a personal search for happiness in relationships and an exploration of women's God-given attributes (Hammond, 2014).

The major purpose of this book is to provide women with a roadmap for action on how to gain, exercise, and keep power. I propose the development, application, and mastery of a *NEW power construct, WomenPower Paradigm,* created by and for women. The Paradigm involves the development and practice of key Character Traits and Core Competencies that are critical in the acquisition and sustainability of individual and collective power. We have to be *ruthlessly strategic, intentional, and systematic* in learning, applying, and mastering this basic framework and its key concepts. In the pages that follow, we will offer you an *empirical framework* on how to gain power, a *systematic process* on how to implement and apply this matrix and related concepts, and share with you real life examples of remarkable women who have succeeded and have mastered the art and practice of leadership and power. This strategic change has to occur at the ***individual, collective,*** and ***systemic*** **levels,** and it has to be guided by the spirit of collaboration, compromise, and support for the greater good of all women aspiring to lead and to change the status quo. According to Congresswoman Lisa Blunt Rochester, women can assist other women to be effective leaders by "advocating for each other, when in the room and when not in the room. We need to be there for each other." Let's minimize competition and conflict, push the seeds of jealousy and envy by the wayside, and focus on common grounds. United by a common purpose, we are stronger together and could have limitless opportunities to gain cohesive and transformative power. **Social innovation is the path; collective power is the goal.**

Introduction

THE DISASTROUS DEFEAT OF HILLARY CLINTON, an experienced and professional woman, to an inexperienced, Machiavellian character of dubious integrity, dealt a crushing blow to women's fight for equality. Decades of struggle have not galvanized enough women—The Vital Many—to unite and claim power that could have resulted in enduring social change. How do we deal with this burning rage that has consumed us since the presidential election of 2016? Do we self-immolate or do we turn it into a teachable moment?

POWER is the critical ingredient and the missing link in our struggle for equality and recognition. When our Founding Fathers drafted the Constitution, the first three words were the most powerful and compelling statement of inclusiveness and equality: "We the People." The power to lead and to govern the country emanates from the people, not from a monarch, not from a president or any head of a nation, but from the people. However, the word "We" does not appear to include women, black people, or Native Americans. Women were not granted the right to vote in America until 1920, 100 years ago. In 2020, women are still struggling to overcome the gender disparity that's endemic in this country. Here are a few examples of this gender gap. According to a study conducted by the Pew Research Center (2017), women make 82 percent of what their male counterparts earn. This means that women have to work an additional 47 days a year to earn as much as men do. Women have not been socialized or trained to compete in competitive sports, and it wasn't until 1972, with the passage of Title IX, that women's participation in sports increased significantly. The Pew Research Center reported that "the share of female CEOs of Fortune 500 companies reached an all-time high of 6.4% in 2017, with 32 women heading major firms. But the share has fallen to 4.8% after several high-profile women left their posts, including Denise Morrison of Campbell Soup Co. and Meg Whitman of Hewlett Packard Enterprise." Although there have been giant steps toward gender parity, women still have major barriers to overcome to achieve a semblance of power and equality. American women are still second-class citizens.

This book offers women and disenfranchised minorities a guideline for action on how to gain, exercise, and keep power. The author proposes the application and development of a NEW power construct—the **WomenPower Paradigm**—that involves the development of key **character traits** and core competencies that are critical in the acquisition and sustainability of individual and collective power. In addition, the author, using a modified **design thinking process**, offers a systematic, deliberate, and focused five-step process as a roadmap to power. The goal is to be intentional and systematic in this collective effort that requires the guidance of an experienced mentor or executive coach and the wisdom of a "kitchen cabinet." Women do not need to reach for the sky to "break the glass ceiling." Our mission, which is right in front of us, is to finally be able to **stand** on the same marble slab and to use our **voices** in the same podium in the White House, the hallowed halls of Congress, and other seats of power that men have claimed for centuries. Together, we can co-create our desired future.

The purpose of this book is twofold. At the **individual level**, it is offered as a guideline for action that has the potential of improving women's abilities to achieve and keep their version of power and influence. At the **societal level**, it's a **social innovation** that's intended to promote positive individual and societal **change** by looking at systemic social issues that challenge society and offer innovative solutions to promote global equity and justice and increase life satisfaction for all.

This book was written for all women who are aspiring to gain and keep power and influence in the workplace, the communities where they live, and the wider world around them.

Methodology: Individual Interviews and Focus Groups

Individual Interviews: Intensive individual interviews of several powerful women were conducted. They were asked to share their experiences concerning their journey toward power and influence; how they developed key competencies and foundational traits to influence others; the circle of people who inspired them to pursue their dreams; and how they faced the challenges and conflicting messages posed by a society that values some but not all of its people. The interviewees also reviewed, analyzed, and provided feedback on the WomenPower Paradigm of power and influence.

Focus Groups: A focus group is a "carefully planned discussion designed to obtain perceptions in a defined area of interest in a permissive and non-threatening environment" (Krueger, 1994). It is a special type of group interview where the moderator creates a safe and nurturing environment that supports differences in opinions and

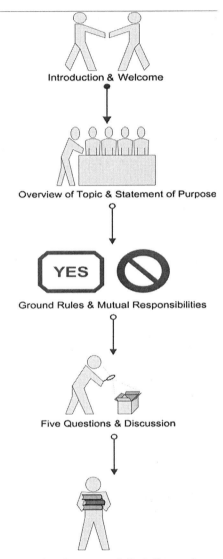

Introduction & Welcome

Overview of Topic & Statement of Purpose

YES

Ground Rules & Mutual Responsibilities

Five Questions & Discussion

Concluding Statement & Path Forward

Figure 1: Focus Group Interview Process

points of view. The moderator assumes a less dominating and directive role, while the subjects or respondents take a more active role by commenting on areas they deem important. The author conducted a statewide focus group based on geographic and demographic identifiers, which included women from Kent, New Castle, and Sussex counties in Delaware. The participants were asked to review and provide feedback on the development of and revisions to the Women-Power Paradigm.

CHAPTER 1

Background Information

Definition of Power:
Machiavellian or WomenPower Paradigm?

IT HAS ALWAYS INTRIGUED ME WHY WOMEN in positions of power appear to either abdicate or abuse power that's granted to them. As an executive coach, I have the opportunity to observe, mentor, and assist women in nurturing and growing their management and leadership skills and their abilities to handle and keep power. In my country of birth, women have always wielded power in the household, in organizations, and in government, so this American role perversion confuses me. Why is there such a confusing and complicated relationship between women and power?

What is power? There are many definitions of power proposed from the time of Machiavelli to the latest monograph on power by the famed historian Mary Beard. The feminist scholar Carolyn Heilbrun (*Writing a Woman's Life*, 1988) defined power as "the ability to take one's place in whatever discourse is essential to action and the right to have one's part matter." For the purpose of this current discussion, let's agree to define **power** as an individual's ability to affect other people's behavior and influence them to act in certain ways. Power is influence-potential and the litmus test of a person's power is getting people to **act** in a specific way. In this definition, we focus attention on action and behavior.

In the classic treatise on power, *The Prince*, Niccolò Machiavelli advised leaders that to keep political power it is better to be cruel than merciful and to be feared rather than loved. Machiavellianism has been inextricably linked to the use of cunning, duplicity, and fear in grabbing and keeping power. It is the power model that has been successfully used by government and business leaders, politicians, and the military. In his best-selling book *The 48 Laws of Power* (2000), Robert Greene expounded on the amoral guidelines for action on how to grab and keep power through conquest and total domination of your competitors or vital others from whom you demand compliance. Below are examples of his effective but ethically questionable strategies for action:

- 2nd Law of Power: Never put too much trust in friends; learn how to use enemies.
- 3rd Law of Power: Conceal your intentions.
- 7th Law of Power: Get others to do the work for you, but always take credit.
- 11th Law of Power: Learn to keep people dependent on you.
- 12th Law of Power: Use selective honesty and generosity to disarm your victim.
- 13th Law of Power: When asking for help, appeal to people's self-interest, never to their mercy or gratitude.
- 15th Law of Power: Crush your enemies totally.

Why not follow these laws? They have been fairly effective in dominating and holding others in chains. You don't need to search deep into history to find a "leader" who has and continues to wield power through force, manipulation, and terror. We have a long list of powerful leaders like Hitler, Stalin, Mussolini, Ferdinand Marcos, Idi Amin, and so on who used Machiavellian ways and followed the principles espoused by Robert Greene.

In the next chapters, we will present to you a new model of power, which we refer to as the WomenPower Paradigm. It is our belief that it is an equally effective model of power, which might even prove to be superior to the unethical garden-variety type of power dominance.

Choosing between these two power models is analogous to choosing between two lovers. The new power model is like a lover who offers comfort, security, commitment, stability, and purpose. Its strength is in its staying power, because it champions the common good. It's like a decent lover who offers the trappings of family, enduring love, and the quiet but good life. In contrast, the old power model offers an exciting and lusty life, replete with adventures, conflict, confrontation, and domination. It's a seductive and fascinating lifestyle of total and intoxicating power and wealth. However, it contains within itself its own seeds of destruction—annihilating greed that's inimical to the interest of the common good, which makes its reign short-lived and unsustainable. It's your choice: WomenPower Paradigm or the Machiavellian/Traditional model?

Chapter 2

Roadmap to Power

Foundational Character Traits and Core Competencies

WHY IS MORE THAN HALF of the American population denied power by virtue of their gender? As of 2017, there were 165.31 million women who were treated as second-class citizens (*Statista,* 2018). How can women gain, wield, and keep personal and collective power? I think a reasonable solution to the power confusion and conflict that women face today is to design a new model of power that takes into account their signature strengths, defines new rules of a fundamentally female construct, and identifies structured steps on how to learn and master the desired skills. I envision the new power model to be positive, collaborative, empowering, and inclusive. This adaptive conceptual framework will enhance and hone women's abilities to gain influence across public, nonprofit, and private sectors in this country and around the world.

Character and Competencies—The Twin Towers: The two major components of the **WomenPower Paradigm** are Character and Competencies.

Character and Maturation—Foundational Traits: Required Elements

Character refers to the moral and emotional characteristics and behavior distinctive to an individual. The four elements that are portrayed in Figure 2 are foundational traits that require focus, attention, and practice for all women aspiring to be effective

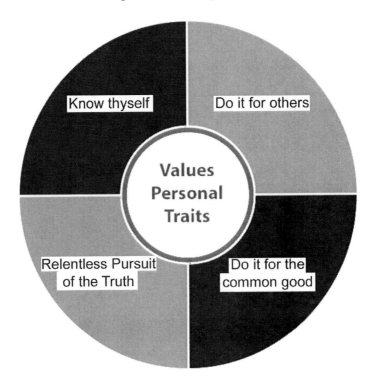

Figure 2: Character and Maturation—Foundational Traits—Women Paradigm

and powerful leaders. The four standard elements—Know Thyself, Do It for Others, Do It for the Common Good, and Pursuit of the Truth—form the framework for personal development and growth. However, the approach to achieving growth and mastery in these areas can vary depending on individual choice. In other words, the "how" and techniques that women use to achieve the goal are non-prescriptive. Personal credibility, ethical and moral character, and principle-driven leadership are stronger attributes in gaining and sustaining the power equilibrium than simply professional competence. Power that's grounded in character and personal credibility has a stronger staying power than one emanating from professional competence.

Know Thyself: Self-Knowledge and Self-Management

Individuals aspiring to gain power have to take time to reflect on who they are, nurture their positive tendencies, and know their values and aspirations. Wayne Muller (1996) believed that within each of us, there is a fundamental core—an essence that captures our true nature. It's only when we possess self-knowledge that we're able to lead and influence others in a beneficent and sustainable way. The following paragraphs are concepts and suggestions that I discussed in my book on happiness entitled, *The Fullness of Nothing: Discover the Hidden Joy That Surrounds You* (2015). The ideas are as relevant to finding happiness as they are to gaining and keeping power.

Self-Knowledge: Knowing who you are, including your strengths and weaknesses, is a critical ingredient to a fulfilling life. The self is fluid and elastic and can be molded and shaped to align and be in harmony with the demands of your ever-changing life. The transitions, opportunities, and possible threats of living and working can be effectively managed if you know your inner voice and your inner core.

In the *Harvard Business Review* article "Managing Oneself" (1999), Peter Drucker counsels us that in order "to do things well, you'll need to cultivate a deeper understanding of yourself—not only what your strengths and weaknesses are, but also how you learn, how you work with others, what your values are, and where you can make the greatest contribution." Self-knowledge and self-management are essential to gaining power and prominence. Below is a short discussion of the seven areas that you need to reflect on in order to succeed in your quest for power:

1. *What are my strengths?* Drucker advises us to have a deep understanding of our strengths in order to use them to the fullest and work on improving them. He states that we don't need to waste valuable time on improving areas of low competence since we're simply moving from mediocrity to average. This step

is critical and will help us know where we belong and where to use our signature strengths so we can make the greatest contribution and enhance our power-potential.

2. *How do I perform?* Are you a listener or a reader? I am a visual learner, and I find it rather challenging to simply listen to a lecture without the benefit of visual aids, such as a PowerPoint presentation, a video, or an easel with written words.

3. *How do I learn?* Do you learn best by listening, writing, or reading? By combining listening to lectures and reading a textbook with note taking, some students have achieved a maximum transfer of learning. Keep this tip in mind as you learn and master the power equation.

4. *What are my values?* Values are ideas about what you consider good, right, and desirable that are manifested in your behavior. Values are deeply embedded in who you are and provide you with a moral compass that guides behavior. Examples of values are moral courage, freedom, loyalty, honesty, integrity, love of family, truth, and justice, to name a few. Sometimes, there is a disconnect between what people think and do, because what you think has not evolved into "values" or what you do as demonstrated by your behavior. Deeply held values become automatic and reflexive as they become part of your subconscious response to situations.

5. "Highly ethical and moral standards category" was selected as the number one top leadership competency by 195 global leaders from 15 countries who were asked to rate 74 qualities (Sunnie Giles, 2016). This survey demonstrates the importance of values, principles, and ethics in building personal and professional credibility. Howard Morgan writes in his book *The Art and Practice of Leadership Coaching* (2005) that "credibility is the foundation of leadership. If we don't believe the messenger, we won't believe the message."

6. *Where do I belong?* Drucker notes that knowing where one belongs is key to success and work satisfaction, because it can transform an ordinary person into an outstanding performer.

If your most cherished value is individual freedom and personal accountability, working in a highly structured hierarchical bureaucracy might not be an appropriate choice for you.

7. *What should I contribute?* Knowing your personal strengths, your way of learning and performing, and your value system, where can you make the greatest contribution? What results have to be achieved to make a difference? If your most cherished values are freedom and creativity, you will flourish in an organization that empowers its workers, nurtures individual creativity, and promotes organizational innovation and learning.

8. *Responsibility for relationships.* Managing yourself requires taking responsibility for relationships within your organization. It's your job to know the strengths, the performance modes, and the value system of your manager and your colleagues. Drucker points out that organizations are built on trust and on confidence in the ability and integrity of people in your organization (Covey, 2006).

Knowing your strengths and weaknesses, your way of learning and performing, your value system, and how you can succeed in the workplace and in your community all contribute to professional and personal satisfaction, which in turn can pave the way for sustaining prestige, prominence, and power.

Do It for Others

When power is used to serve and benefit others, it becomes synergistic. Research has shown (Keltner, 2017) that power is wielded most effectively when it is used by individuals who are aware of the needs and wants of the people it benefits. This style of power is vastly more effective than the use of fear, deception, and force. Keltner contends that power is conferred to individuals who are compassionate, respectful, empathetic, and grateful rather than when grabbed through brute force and fear. Although most people gain power by enhancing the lives of others, once they gain power, they oftentimes forget to practice the core behaviors that got them into positions of power. Power goes to their heads. It's intoxicating, which eventually leads them to use power for their own personal promotion and benefit.

What motivates people to help others? There are times when individuals help others because they expect something in return, which is referred to as the norm of reciprocity in social psychology. It is an intrinsic motivator, where recipients feel indebted to return the favor granted by helpers. Recent research (Van Tongeren, et al., 2016) indicates that a more powerful force is the extrinsic motivator—empathy-altruistic norm—where leaders understand, appreciate, and are sensitive to what others are going through because they experience vicariously what the recipients are feeling. When leaders focus on other people's needs, they then are less inclined to focus on themselves.

Do It for the Common Good: The Norm of Social Responsibility

Social responsibility is an ethical framework that suggests that an entity, be it an organization or an individual, has the obligation to act for the benefit of society or for the common good. According to Jim Wallis (2013), "the notion of the common good has both religious and secular roots going back to Catholic social teaching, the Protestant social gospel, Judaism, Islam, and in the American Constitution itself, which says that government should promote the general welfare." He remarked that an authentic commitment to the common good could bring our divided nation together to address our most serious and systemic challenges, such as health care, immigration, and gun violence.

When leaders use power to promote the common good, they find common grounds to safeguard the sustainability of our society for the good of all. This approach is one of the most effective ways of exercising and keeping power.

Figure 3: Maslow's Hierarchy of Needs—Using to Self-Actualize

What motivates us to get up, live, and work every single day? Psychologist Abraham Maslow proposed that individuals seek to satisfy five basic needs: physiological, safety, social, esteem, and self-actualization. He noted that the lowest level of unmet needs is the prime motivator and that these needs must be satisfied before individuals move to the higher-level needs. Once an unmet need is satisfied, they then are able to move to the next level. An analysis of the three components of Character Development and Maturation indicates that all three relate to higher-level needs of self-esteem, self-actualization, and transcendence. Self-esteem needs include the need to feel good about oneself and one's capabilities, to be respected by others, and to receive recognition and appreciation. Self-actualization needs include the need and ability to realize one's full potential as a human being, including helping others (Transcendence).

Relentless Pursuit of the Truth

What is the truth? Is there a Universal Truth? How do we know it's the truth? The truth is pure, unadorned, unembellished, and sacred. The truth is naked, unadulterated, and transcendent. Merriam-Webster defines the truth as "the body of real things, events, and facts: actuality." This element rises to the top at this time in our nation's history because our leaders have not demonstrated moral courage in their pursuit of the truth. The leaders of the most powerful country in the world, both the former top executive and a majority of members of Congress, have a tenuous attachment to the truth. We had a leader who deliberately lied, unable to tell the difference between truth and fiction, and continues to attack our freedoms. The American people are confused and are hungry for a leader who can elevate our spirits from the profane to the sublime, unite us with a worthy goal and vision, and restore our faith in our leaders. I suspect that the dysfunction at the top is simply a symptom of a stunning national malaise that is endemic at every level of our society. Of course, this is an assumption that could be the subject of another major research project. Consider the following ethical dilemmas that often occur in the workplace (Sam McKeeman, 2012):

- Leader X hired an employee over another, better qualified one, because she is a friend, and she knows his ways better than the other candidate.
- Leader Y frequently leaves the office for an afternoon meeting that typically ends before the end of the work day, and then proceeds to go directly home.
- Employee A uses the office copier for personal reasons, such as making photocopies of his income tax return, a school term paper, or an email message to a friend.
- Leader Z claimed an award that she does not deserve, as portrayed in the narrative below: Her employees did all the work, but she got the credit.

The final example is an account of an ethical violation, granted not an illegal one, that a friend witnessed a couple of years ago.

Connie, the manager of a small IT company, just won the local Chamber of Commerce Innovator of the Year Award in a small town in the northeastern United States. Her team, however, was furious about it. They all felt that the team leader, Sabrina, should have gotten the award. She planned, designed, tested, and successfully implemented the GIS application. The team assisted her in designing and testing the prototype and supported her efforts to improve the initial application. Their client, the local hospital, was delighted with the project outcome, which was completed two years before Connie was hired. The entire team felt deflated and unappreciated. Connie justified accepting the award because she felt she was promoting the company, not herself. How would you feel if you were Sabrina? Is this fair and equitable? Is Connie's justification aligned with the truth? This and many more scenarios like this are typical and systemic in our current society, where doublespeak is common and people are confused about facts, lies, and the truth. Leaders who wield power have to be vigilant and serve as role models to the rest of the organization and the community. Most people do not start out abusing power. It happens over time. How do we regain the truth and prevent ourselves from descending into the same black hole?

Ethics, its practical application, and subsequent dilemmas are common occurrences that we face on a daily basis. As parents, we need to get actively involved in the character development of our children and in imparting concepts of what's right and what's wrong in terms of ethical behavior. Ethical principles might need to be taught not only at home, but also in schools, in communities, and in the workplace. Ethics refers to standards of behavior that tell us how human beings ought to act in the many situations that they find themselves in—as friends, parents, citizens, workers, professionals, business people, and so on (Velasquez, Andre, Shanks & Meyer, 2010). It is a set of *moral principles* or values, such as truth, respect for life, freedom, and fairness. A little more than a hundred years ago, Lord Moulton, a noted English jurist, defined ethics as *"obedience to the unenforceable."* In an article published in 1924 in the *Atlantic Monthly*, Lord Moulton divided human action into three domains:

positive law, absolute choice, and "manners." At one extreme is the domain of law, where "our actions are prescribed by laws binding upon us which must be obeyed." At the other extreme is the domain of free choice, which "includes all those actions as to which we claim and enjoy full freedom." In between these two extremes is the ethical domain, where our actions are not determined by law, but we are also not free to behave in any way we choose. In the ethical domain, Lord Moulton noted that "the true test is the extent to which individuals composing the nation can be trusted to obey self-imposed law." Below is a graphic representation of Lord Moulton's concept of the ethical domain as "obedience to the unenforceable."

For those of you who wield power, be relentless in your pursuit of the Universal Truth, especially when it affects the vulnerable, the disadvantaged, the powerless, and, ultimately, the common good.

How would you rate yourself when it comes to ethics? Which of the following best applies to you?

1. I am always ethical
2. I am mostly ethical
3. I am somewhat ethical
4. I am seldom ethical
5. I am never ethical

Industrial engineer and futurist Marvin Cetron posed the following ethical dilemma to business students several decades ago

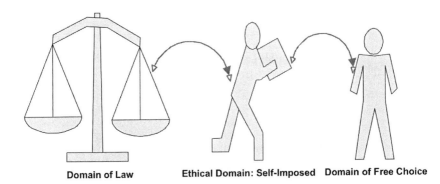

Domain of Law   Ethical Domain: Self-Imposed   Domain of Free Choice

Figure 4: Ethical Domain—Obedience to the Unenforceable

(McKeeman, 2012): "If you could do an illegal deal, get caught and tried and convicted, and serve a three-year prison sentence, but emerge with $500 million from the deal, would you do it?" He reported that three in five students replied "absolutely." Although this example is an exaggeration of an ethical dilemma that could challenge our moral compass, it's a hypothetical example that catches the audience's attention and shows what ordinary people are capable of doing for the *almighty dollar*. When I posed the same question to a group of specialists working with people with disabilities, approximately 60 percent were willing to go to jail if they could come out with a $500 million payback.

Values and Beliefs

The major drivers for all four character components are beliefs and values. Beliefs refer to what we think, while values are how we act, as demonstrated by our behavior. Sometimes, there is a disconnect between our collective ideals and visions and our imperfect and dysfunctional realities. The disconnect happens when beliefs have not been successfully internalized and hard-wired into our subconscious. For example, a majority of our political leaders pay lip service and pledge to use their power and influence to promote the welfare of ordinary citizens. In practice, not long after being sworn into office, some of them start using their power to pay off political debts to the power elites, their supporters, family and friends, and other vested interests. The will and commitment to serve and to help others and to promote the common good are summarily forgotten. The myopia of power and its intoxicating vapors have set in. Trusting in our better angels is not a reliable practice. Character development, training, and practice need to be a continuing effort in order to sustain the effective and ethical use of power and influence. Instilling the right beliefs and values are the major drivers of this ethical framework, spiced with knowledge, practice, and vigilance.

Case Study: Malala Yousafzai—
A Young Woman of Character and Substance

Malala Yousafzai is a Pakistani education advocate and social activist who at age 17 became the youngest person to win the Nobel Peace Prize. She defied the Taliban's prohibition on the education of girls, which in turn made her a target of the Taliban's wrath and indignation. On October 9, 2012, Malala was shot by a Taliban gunman while she was traveling on a school bus on her way home. She survived the vicious attack and was flown from Peshwar, Pakistan, to Birmingham, England, for surgery and further treatment. This violent incident was the tipping point that awakened the world's consciousness to the systemic problem of denying girls the right to education. Gordon Brown, the United Nations' special envoy for global education, introduced a petition for all children around the world to have the right to education by 2015. Pakistani president Asif Ali Zardari announced the creation of the country's first Right to Education Bill and the launch of a $10 million education fund in Malala's honor. The Vital Voices Global Partnership also established a Malala Fund to support education for all girls all around the world.

How can someone so young and vulnerable achieve such great feats in a relatively short period of time? How did Malala develop such courage and wisdom in the face of adversity and a firm resolve to forge ahead despite the danger? How did she gain the tenacity and focus to achieve her life's purpose?

Malala, by any definition, is a remarkable young woman—a powerful and great leader who influenced a social innovation by the strength of her conviction and will. She single-handedly redefined the rights of women and girls to free and quality education. She appears to possess the foundational character traits and attributes that we discussed earlier in this book. She has a deep understanding of her strengths, which she used to advocate for her cause. At age 11, using the pseudonym Gul Makai, she started blogging about life in Pakistan under the repressive regime of the Taliban. In 2013, she wrote the international bestseller, *I Am Malala: The Girl Who Stood Up and Was Shot by the Taliban*. That same year, she won the

United Nations Human Rights Prize, which is awarded to a deserving recipient only every five years, and was named *Time* magazine's most influential person for 2013. To date, at age 21, she has received more than 40 awards and honors for her courage, advocacy, and relentless pursuit of her mission to help others, and to serve and promote the common good.

Paulo Coelho, bestselling author of *The Alchemist* (1988), proclaims that "to realize one's destiny is a person's only obligation." It appears that at the young age of 13, Malala had already achieved her personal legend, her calling in life. The story of Malala is a remarkable testament to the decisive importance of character, self-knowledge, service to others, and relentless pursuit of what is good and right as critical ingredients in gaining and keeping power. She's comfortable speaking the truth and using her transformative power and influence to spark universal change that benefits all.

Eight Core Competencies:
Recommended Electives

Competencies refer to the ability or capacity of individuals to do a job successfully and efficiently. To be competent, they must exhibit patterns of behavior that distinguish high performance when compared with those engaged in the same or comparable tasks or roles in a similar work environment. Professional competence alone is not sufficient to endow leaders with power; however, incompetent leaders have unlimited opportunities to fail and to suffer the loss of power. The eight core competencies presented in Figure 5 are suggested areas of proficiency for women who are attempting to learn the ways of the powerful. The list is based on a literature review of current research, the expert recommendations from powerful women we interviewed, and responses from a select group of women and men from diverse backgrounds, who comprised the design team involved in drafting the WomenPower Paradigm.

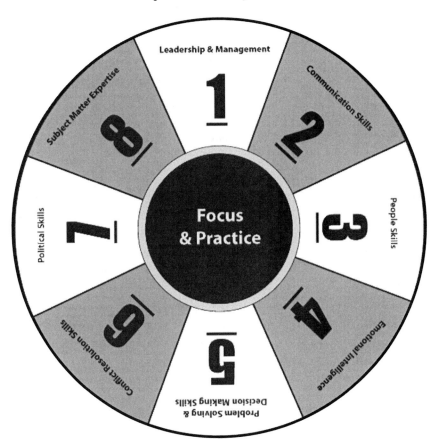

Figure 5: Core Competencies of Powerful Women—WomenPower Paradigm

Leadership and Management: Learning to Lead from Any Position

It is my belief that before women can lead others, they have to know who they are and how to manage themselves in both their private and public lives. What do I mean by managing yourself? First and foremost, women need to learn the skills of self-awareness and self-knowledge. For example, a colleague of mine is coaching a woman who does not have a good feel for who she is, what her strengths and weaknesses are, her value system, and how she can improve her skills. She thinks she knows, but invariably she makes the same mistakes that her coach pointed out to her in previous sessions. There appears to be a gap between her academic knowledge and its practical, hands-on application. She is hard working and fairly competent, but her skills, competencies, and values are not aligned with the mission, vision, and operating values of the organization that she works for. Given her strength, her innovative spirit, but her inability to work with a team and her lack of emotional intelligence, she could make a greater contribution in another industry, possibly an IT firm.

It is also critical for women to possess the skills and competencies of effective management and leadership. Oftentimes, articles and books on organizational development value and better appreciate the contributions of leaders more than managers. As management expert John O'Leary noted, "Business people and business theorists love to draw distinctions between management and leadership. They tell us that managers do things right; leaders do the right things and management is administration, but leadership is innovation." He argues that "certain behaviors and activities are common to the effective administration of both leadership and management" and that the only difference is "the focus of the person carrying them out." In practice, he concludes, "focus more on people, and you'll demonstrate leadership, more on results, you'll perform management."

My personal philosophy is that to be a consummate leader and to gain and keep power, women need to learn the skills and capabilities of both managers and leaders. Managers plan and organize people, money, and resources in order to achieve outcomes. They build organizational structures and draft policies and guidelines for action, stability, and order. Leaders inspire and motivate people to action and to achieve a collective vision of a preferred future. It's a symbiotic relationship between these two functions, where leaders need managers and managers need leaders to achieve the mission and vision of the organization. You can't do one without the other, not unless you're high up in the pecking order, where you have a cabinet or capable leadership team doing the managing and leading. Learning and honing your skills in both areas will equip you to successfully "lead" and wield power from any position and in different arenas of life.

Communication Skills: Great Communicator

Women aspiring to gain and keep power must understand the importance and benefits of practicing effective communication and active listening skills. It is critical to building and sustaining relationships, influence skills, and organizational effectiveness. **Interpersonal communication** is the sharing of information between two or more individuals to reach a common understanding (George, Jones & Hill, 1998). The focus of this current discussion is on face-to-face communication. How do we spend our communication time? According to human resource expert and author Peter R. Garber (2008), we spend 16 percent of our time reading, 9 percent writing, 30 percent talking, and 45 percent listening. It appears that to be an effective communicator we need to develop and nurture our listening skills, in addition to practicing our speaking skills. Given that our **attention span** is less than that of a goldfish (*Time*, 2015), we need to listen more effectively to better understand and reflect on the key points that others are saying. Our attention span has decreased to eight seconds from 12 seconds in 2000; in comparison, the attention span of a goldfish is nine seconds. To complicate matters, our **retention rate** is 17 seconds, and even less than that for younger folks at 10 seconds. To further test our listening skills, we think faster than we speak. We speak at a rate of 150 words per minute, but we process information (hearing and thinking) at 1000 words per minute. This huge gap gives us plenty of time to go on a mental excursion someplace else, rather than listening to what's being said. Hence, the need and importance of empathetic listening and conveying concise, clear, and accurate messages.

It's also important to remember that interpersonal communication effectiveness can be learned. Although some people appear to have a natural talent, an inborn tendency to excel at communicating, it is a skill that can be learned, practiced, and strategically managed.

Having effective interpersonal communication skills is comparable to having extraordinary talent in athletics or writing, but those who don't possess the innate talent can learn to be competent athletes and writers. Likewise, some people have an aptitude for communicating, like former president Ronald Reagan, but others can also learn to be competent communicators.

Emotional and Social Intelligence

I have the good fortune of working with an individual who appears to remain confident, unabashed and resolute, even under the most trying circumstances, and handles the most compromising social situations with grace and determination. At the young age of 36, she was the top executive of several state departments, and a decade later, she was voted the first African American Congresswoman for a small state in the northeastern United States. Renowned psychologist and best-selling author Daniel Goleman would refer to such a leader as possessing high emotional intelligence or EI. Emotional intelligence refers to the ability to identify and manage one's emotions and monitor those of others, and use emotional information to guide thinking and behavior (Peter Salovey & John Mayer, 1990). Experts agree that this type of intelligence plays an important role in leadership success, although a causal correlation between the two variables has not been established. Daniel Goleman, in partnership with Richard Boyatzis (2013), suggests that there are four critical domains to the Emotional and Social Intelligence Leadership model. These domains include the following:

- Self-Awareness: refers to the ability to recognize and to understand our emotions and their effects on our performance.
- Self-Management: refers to the ability to regulate and manage our emotions and express them appropriately, depending on the context and situation. This does not mean that we have to suppress our emotions; it only means that we need to

identify the suitable time, place, and situation to express them appropriately and effectively.

- Social Awareness: the ability to interact well with others, to sense their feelings and perspectives, and to put ourselves in another person's shoes. To communicate and connect effectively with people, it's critical that we understand and vicariously experience their feelings and thoughts.
- Relationship Management: the ability to have a positive influence on others and gain their support and confidence.

Several years ago, I was hired to coach a young woman, who has had relative success in working in a small organization in a specific but delimited area of responsibility. When she received a promotion to a leadership role, she failed miserably. I was puzzled by this unexpected outcome, since she is highly intelligent, a gifted and competent professional, and highly trained in leadership and organizational development. To top it all, she has a beautiful heart and a sharp mind. After months of working with her, I realized that in addition to her lack of experience as a leader and manager, she also has low emotional and social intelligence. She was unable to read the non-verbal cues from her staff, her leadership team, and partners that she collaborated with. Consequently, she hired the wrong people and surrounded herself with spineless yes-men, resulting in chaos and confusion.

People Skills: Interpersonal Skills

This competency is a sub-set of the social intelligence skill that we discussed earlier. It is key to gaining and keeping power, because we need to understand people's personalities and behavior to build effective and lasting relationships. Individuals with strong interpersonal skills are able to play different roles with different types of people and know how to best fit in and get along. My son Joe is the quintessential "social being" with great people skills. He is able to carry on friendly and interesting conversations with the governor as comfortably as he could with the janitor of his building. He is well-liked by his family, his peers, his friends and sometimes, even by his enemies. It's the same story with Jackie, who wins the "Ms. Congeniality Award" at her office. Employees, supervisors, and clients all adore her.

Decision Making and Problem-Solving Skills

I find that one of the most pressing problems that women friends and acquaintances of mine encounter in their daily lives today is their inability to solve problems and make decisions. I know someone who talks about the same decade-old problems again and again, but has no clue on how to resolve them. It appears to be endemic among women managers I have worked with or have coached in the past. Either they fail to see the problem or they fail to take steps to resolve them, because they're unable to make decisions due to lack of information and knowledge. I often wonder if these are issues that a majority of women in our society are confronted with. With training, dedication, and practice, problem-solving and decision-making skills could be learned and applied to the daily challenges of life and work.

Critical thinking to solve problems and make crucial decisions is a required skill for today's professionals. With organizations running "leaner and meaner," individual contributors, managers, and executives alike need to understand how to methodically, strategically, and collaboratively make decisions, solve problems, and foster innovation. In today's workplace, leaders are faced with complex and pressing problems that need to be addressed and resolved. There are some instances when they have the luxury of time to collect relevant data and information before making a decision, but many times, they have to make an intuitive decision on the spot. I have often suggested to leaders that they form a leadership team, charged with the responsibility of giving them advice and guidance and providing relevant and reliable data to help them make enlightened decisions. The following are steps that I have used in my practice to make decisions about a course of action:

1. Problem: Define the problem, issue, or challenge
2. Goals: State the goals clearly and accurately
3. Data: Collect current, reliable, and relevant data (vital few)
4. Solutions: List alternative solutions, compare and contrast solutions, and choose one solution
5. Action: Take action on your choice
6. Assess: Review, follow-up, and assess your choice

Is it better to use our minds or our hearts when making critical, high-stakes decisions? It all depends on the situation, the complexity and ramifications of the problem, the time frame, and other situational variables. However, in the majority, it is best to use a logical method to address problems of a strategic nature. Never, ever make a decision out of anger or jealousy or when you're motivated by negative emotions. Cool down, clear your head, and silence that cascading flow of uncontrollable and unconscious emotions. Sleep on it, collect your thoughts, appeal to your better self, get in sharper focus, and logically map out your platform. Stand ready to be deliberate, intentional, fair, and logical.

Conflict Management Skills

Conflict is inevitable in any human interaction and endemic in a society that espouses competition rather than collaboration and support. In the competition equation, when one person fails, the other person wins, a divisive principle that encourages conflict in every facet of American life—in sports, in the workplace, in schools, and in neighborhoods. Competition is celebrated as a cherished value and is an animating force that motivates the American psyche. No wonder conflict is everywhere, especially in the current political climate. Conflict management and resolution skills are therefore more crucial than ever in managing differences and preventing them from escalating into full-blown violence and destruction.

Conflict management involves helping employees, colleagues,

and others to prevent or to resolve conflicts and to adjudicate between two parties through compromise or collaboration (win-win) techniques. It also involves the ability to manage and resolve our own conflict situations, such as disagreements with employees, managers, neighbors, friends, and other crucial relationships. Or a president, uniting a divided, confused, and battered country by painting a moral vision of things to come and having the audacity to act on it. The powerful and courageous have the ability to win over people through a message of hope, tolerance, and inclusion. It is challenging to gain and keep power when individuals are unable to manage relationships effectively, tolerate differences, keep primal emotions in check, and practice tenacity and patience. However, there are instances when individuals have to cut their losses by facing problems and confronting issues that have been plaguing a typically trusting relationship. For example, a wife needs to confront an unfaithful husband to save a marriage, or the manager must let the non-performing employee go to save the sagging staff morale and to stop wasting limited dollars.

Political Skills

Political competency is essential and one of the most critical ingredients to gaining and wielding power, yet it's the least understood and most feared and avoided by those attempting to gain power. Bacharach, author of the book *Get Them on Your Side: Win Support, Convert Skeptics, Get Results* (2006), remarks, "For too long, it has remained in the closet. It's one of the competencies that everyone needs—but nobody talks about." Politics and political skills of leaders is a contentious topic because most people think of the skill in negative terms, like "political machinations" and "dirty political tricks." Politics is simply the science and the art of government and political principles. It's when individuals manipulate the system for their own self-promotion that politics becomes partisan, negative, manipulative, and devious. In other words, it morphs into its Machiavellian face.

What is political skill? A review of existing literature shows that there are many definitions of political skill and no consensus on what it really means. Professor Gerald Ferris of Florida State University defines political skill as "the ability to understand and effectively influence others for personal or organizational benefits." To me this does not define political skills, it is simply a definition of power. Professor Bacharach from Cornell University suggests that "it's the ability to understand what you can and cannot control, when to take action, who is going to resist your agenda, and whom you need on your side. It's about knowing how to map the political terrain and get others on your side, as well as lead coalitions." Interesting definition, although it fails to focus on "what" political skill is; rather the definition provides us with the "how" of the political skill spectrum. Let me offer an operational definition that I will use as a guide in this discussion on political power and competency: *political skill is the ability to understand and influence the power structure within an organization, a community, or the larger society in order to achieve personal, collective, or organizational goals.* It is rather challenging to define the skill without including the power definition (influence-potential) because political skill sits on the same throne as power. In fact, it's the quickest and possibly the most direct route to power.

Structure of Power: How do individuals identify the structure of power in a community? What are proven strategies that might lead them to the inner sanctum of power and influence? Sociologist Ashley Crossman (2019) defines power structure as "the distribution of power among individuals or among social categories or entire social systems, such as groups, organizations, communities or societies." According to Floyd Hunter (1953), a small homogeneous group of upper class elite dominates and controls power within a community. Hunter was an American social worker and sociologist and the author of the seminal book *Community Power Structure: A Study of Decision Makers* (1953). He examined in detail the distribution of decision-making and power in a regional city and concludes that powerful decision makers are concentrated in a relatively stable upper class. Three years later, another sociologist, C. Wright Mills, suggested that the "power elite" dominates the national agenda and decision making in Washington, D.C. A more recent study by G. William Domhoff (2005) presents convincing evidence that power in America is dominated by a fixed group of privileged people and corporations. Outlined below are his startling and disturbing conclusions on the rule of the powerful elite that dominates both the American economy and government:

- "The rich" coalesce into a social upper class that has developed institutions by which the children of its members are socialized into an upper class worldview, and newly wealthy people are assimilated.
- Members of this upper class control corporations, which have been the primary mechanisms for generating and holding wealth in the United States for upwards of 150 years now.
- There exists a network of nonprofit organizations through which members of the upper class and hired corporate leaders not yet in the upper class shape policy debates in the United States.
- Members of the upper class, with the help of their high-level employees in profit and nonprofit institutions, are able to dominate the federal government in Washington.
- These rich corporate leaders nonetheless claim to be relatively powerless.
- Working people have less power than in many other democratic countries.

Strategies on How to Identify the Seat of Power in a Community: Floyd Hunter (1963) suggests the use of two methods: The first is the *reputational approach,* where the researcher asks a group of informants knowledgeable about the target community to list individuals whom they feel are influential within the community. Various methods could be employed in the selection of informants and the design of the questionnaire; however, one common procedural step is to tally the number of times that an individual is included in the list, and those whose names are mentioned with the greatest frequency form the core of the community power structure. The second method is the *position approach,* where there is an assumption that individuals holding the highest office in the community form the nucleus of the power elites. It's based on the stratification model of position power. By scanning the list of political, economic, and social organizations and entities within the community, the researcher could readily collect the names of the highest-ranking executives in leadership positions and compile a list of the members of the power structure. Of course, these two methods fail to take into consideration individuals who hold informal positions of power by virtue of their personalities or achievements.

Three Phases of Mastering Political Skill: Professor Bacharach offers a three-phase sequential process to learn and master this crucial skill.

- *Map your political terrain:* Identify the specific system that you intend to penetrate and influence; identify the stakeholders and anticipate their positions on the ideas you're presenting; and be prepared to compromise.
- *Get others on your side:* In the current high-tech, information society, where complexity rules, problems, solutions, and new ideas are impossible to resolve or address without the support and guidance of a working team. Building a coalition of individuals with diverse interest and competencies, who are vested in achieving similar goals, is a requirement for success.
- *Make things happen:* The effective exercise of political skill requires action by a critical mass of supporters and allies. To gain support and buy-in, the skilled political leader must appeal to the group's value system and make certain that members are aware that there is a pay-off for their support and allegiance. Stand ready to answer the key question paramount in their minds: "What's in it for me?"

Political behavior, politics, and hierarchy of power exist in all organizations and systems. It's omnipresent in every facet of life, and if we want to get things done, we cannot afford to turn a blind eye to the political dynamics that are happening around us. Just like any skill, political competence can be learned and sharpened through training, experience, and practice.

Competence or Subject Matter Expertise

As we discussed in the beginning of this section, competencies refer to the ability or capacity of individuals to do a job successfully and efficiently. We also stated that professional competence alone is not sufficient to endow leaders with power; however, incompetent leaders have unlimited opportunities to fail and to suffer the loss of power. Knowledge is power—a principle that was as true then as it is relevant today, and even more so in an information society. Being competent does not imply that individuals need to be subject matter experts in all areas of operations, fields of knowledge, or disciplines. To have professional competence and deep understanding of the organization's major products or services, however, is a big plus that builds trust, loyalty, and influence. A focus on professional competencies and skill development contribute to superior performance, which then leads to the accretion of power and influence. As Thomas Kolditz noted in his book *In Extremis Leadership* (2007), "most leaders have gotten to their station in life through their own competence, but that becomes lost on followers unless the leader's competence is occasionally revealed by action. Leaders need to take time and effort to show followers what they're good at and why followers should be confident in the leader's ability." Competence engenders trust in the leader's ability and ultimately endows the leader with influence and power.

Let's examine the quandary that the former president was faced with because a majority of Americans did not feel that he had the competency to lead the country. In a Quinnipiac Survey conducted in 2017, a clear majority (55 percent) of respondents indicated that they thought President Trump was not a good leader. Bear in mind that leading was his most critical task as president. Latest Gallup Poll approval ratings also showed that he was the most unpopular president since 1937. His average approval rating was 39 percent, with the highest approval rating of 45 percent, and the lowest approval rating of *33 percent.* In comparison, President Obama's average approval rating was 47.9 percent, with the highest approval rating of 69 percent, and the lowest approval rating of 38 percent (Wikipedia: United States

Presidential Approval Ratings). Professional competence is a prerequisite for quality governance and authentic leadership, much like our need for oxygen to be able to breathe. Incompetence results in mistrust, chaos, and a divided and disenchanted populace.

Focus and Practice: Lifelong Learning

The animating force that drives the process of learning these eight competencies is relentless focus on the goal. Practice seals the deal. It sharpens and hones our newly acquired skills and competencies. It's fairly easy to get distracted in our Internet-driven society, where our attention is diverted to email messages, social media ringing its seductive call, and big data in the palm of our hands. How do we manage these distractions and focus on our priorities and the task at hand?

When I was deputy director of a fairly large state agency, I had a long list of priorities that I needed to accomplish daily, including long-term projects that were screaming for attention. I also did private consultations and raised two sons as a single parent. I had a checklist, organized in three buckets and listed according to priorities, which forced me to do the important tasks first, even though I might not have enjoyed doing them, such as grant writing. Now that I am working full-time as a consultant, I manage my two big projects using the same checklist-priority strategy. I do my book writing on Friday evenings and weekends, and I do my creative thinking, my open awareness moments, when I take my walks and exercise on my treadmill. I realize that I need more free time to empty my mind, let it run free and unchain it from my tightly structured, regimented life. I go on vacations twice a year and leave the books, the gadgets, and the mind, and let my wild side soar free.

Daniel Goleman (*The Focused Leader*, 2013) defines focus as "thinking about one thing while filtering our distractions." He classified three different modes of attention: focusing on yourself through self-awareness and self-management; focusing on others, which is the foundation of empathy and the ability to build social relationships; and focusing on the wider world that allows leaders to make strategic decisions that affect not only their organizations but also the larger society. He noted that "a primary task of leadership is to direct attention," and to keep in mind that focus is not only an essential leadership skill but also a useful tool in elevating the quality of our daily lives. Our ability to focus and to pay attention affects every facet of our lives and "ripples through most everything we seek to accomplish," including learning and mastering the competencies to be powerful leaders.

Case Study: Margaret Thatcher

Character: Foundational Traits: Margaret Thatcher will be remembered in history as the first female prime minister of the United Kingdom, who was elected to office on May 3, 1979. She served as prime minister from 1979 through 1990 and as leader of the Conservative Party from 1975 through 1990. She had a strong set of values and principles, instilled in her by her father, Alfred Roberts, a Methodist lay-preacher and a small business owner. She was a devout Methodist, with strong moral ethics and conviction. She recalled in the book *The Path to Power* (1995) that she went to Sunday School in the morning before accompanying her parents to service, and went back again to Sunday school in the afternoon. It appears that institutionalized religion had a major influence on young Margaret's socialization and character building. She grew up in a small town in Grantham, Lincolnshire, where she learned the values of duty, neighborliness and civic pride, and appreciated the generosity and norm of social responsibility practiced by members of the Rotary. She was firm and resolute in her convictions, because she was guided by unchanging values and beliefs that were instilled in her from early childhood through her family, her community, and her religion.

Competencies: Thatcher's leadership style has been described by political analysts as autocratic, forceful, and non-participative. Autocratic leaders tend to be self-confident, forceful, and at times uncompromising in achieving their goals and visions. This type of leadership is needed during crisis situations, when focused decision making and quick action are crucial. However, when the crisis is over and transition to stability and normalcy is secure, the autocratic, forceful, and non-participative approach becomes less effective. Kaiser and Kaplan (2013) pointed out in the article "Thatcher's Greatest Strength Was Her Greatest Weakness," that "it was her trademark grit, determination, ideological certainty, and scorn for consensus politics that drove her political achievements—privatization and the revitalization of the British economy, full repudiation of the socialist experiment, standing up to the tyranny of the Soviet Union.... But it was overdoing those strengths that made Thatcher so divisive. She could be obstinate, stubborn, uncompromising...."

Thatcher was politically savvy, a competent and decisive leader and a good communicator. Her father, Alfred Roberts, had a dominant influence in the prime minister's life, as confirmed in her book *The Path to Power* (1995). She remarked that "perhaps the main interest which my father and I shared while I was a girl was a thirst for knowledge about politics and public affairs." She knew how to navigate the invisible power structure, because she had been socialized to work and prosper within the political structure through her father, who was active in that arena. Later in life, her husband Denis Thatcher's vital support and wealth allowed her entrance into a powerful social class that endowed her with prestige, status, and the freedom to engage in politics as a full-time career. Baroness Thatcher was also a trained chemist and lawyer, who specialized in tax law, which provided her with a strong background when dealing with finance legislation.

Margaret Thatcher was a great and transformational leader. She was a pioneer, who learned and mastered the rules of the power game with steely determination and grit. Although she did not set out to serve as a role model for women, she stood victorious in achieving most of the goals she wanted to accomplish, despite the strong opposition from the male establishment and the absence of support from other women. Her leadership style served her well, because it was the appropriate style needed by the weakened United Kingdom at that time—where the economy was in shambles, foreign investment needed to be revitalized, and the country's world influence was at a low ebb. Although Thatcher was not a leader for all seasons, she opened the bolted golden door to public service, power, and leadership for all women for many years to come.

CHAPTER 3

Roadmap to Power

A Five-Step Process

CULTURE OF POWER: The journey to power requires fundamental changes both at the individual and societal levels. This section will provide you with systematic and replicable steps to gain and keep power. The culture of power at the societal level requires additional research and testing and could be the subject of another book. With focus and practice, mastery is possible, and with mastery comes comfort and control. Someday, it will be part of who you are; it will become part of your unconscious mind.

Culture consists of beliefs, values, behaviors, and material objects that constitute a people's way of life (Macionis, 1998). Culture represents a shared way of life that gives us messages that shape our beliefs, perceptions, values, and judgments about who we are, how we relate to others, and how we behave within a society. It is a powerful element and at times is manifested in unconscious and reflexive ways.

I was born and raised in the Philippines and didn't immigrate to this country until I was in my early twenties. The Philippine society is a matriarchy, where women hold and exercise considerable power in running the government and their families, which has led to the birth of strong, dominant, assertive, and at times aggressive women. I was also blessed to have a mom who believed in me and nourished the positive abilities and strength of character that have become part of who I am. Leadership, management, and power have always been an essential part of my upbringing and early life. From the time I was four or five years old, I was taught how to give directions and delegate responsibilities to my nanny, Pining, who helped raise me and took charge of my daily needs. I also had to make sure that the cook, Mrs. Bautista, knew what my favorite dishes were, so she didn't have to guess what satisfied my palate. When my sister Lennie and I were teenagers, my parents delegated to us the responsibility of collecting rent for apartment buildings that we owned. From that assignment, I learned how to manage a small business, how to negotiate with diplomacy and tact, and how to complete an assigned task effectively and efficiently.

From my dad, I learned the values of integrity, principled leadership, and how to interact with the powerful and influential. My dad used to go hunting for ducks and quails in the jungles of Mindoro with President Ramon Magsaysay, who was the seventh president of the Philippines. His greatest achievement was the defeat of the Communist-led Hukbalahap in the Philippines in the mid–1950s. I distinctly remember sitting on his lap as a young child, while he was chatting with my dad and a handful of other journalists. Before we left, he handed me a silver peso, which I kept as a souvenir and which further inspired me to start collecting coins. There were also regular visits from my dad's peers from the *Philippines Free Press*, *The Herald*, and other publications. Renowned and respected journalists gathered in our living room, discussing national events, literature, philosophy, and the like. I was like a sponge, absorbing the scintillating conversations of these erudite men and some women. I learned and practiced power, influence, management, and leadership at home from my parents and their friends and acquaintances. My early socialization and identity imprinting to wielding and keeping power happened early and continuously from youth through adulthood. I am comfortable with power, because it has always been part of my behavioral repertoire and my identity.

Now, let's fast-forward to an alien culture, the American society, where I immigrated as a young bride of a college professor. As a first-generation immigrant, I leaned heavily on my cultural heritage to make meaning out of the confusion and identity crisis I experienced when dealing with new ways of behaving and new patterns of behavior in my adopted country.

The 1970s were pivotal years for the American woman. The

Women's Rights Movement exploded in the seventies—women demanded equal rights under the law and revolted against the dominance of men and the open repression of women. The Equal Rights Amendment (ERA) was passed by Congress on March 22, 1971, but failed ratification by the states. It died a natural death by inaction in 1982, when it failed to achieve ratification by a minimum of 38 states.

In the previous decade, President Kennedy signed legislation establishing the President's Commission for Women, which published a report recommending improvements in fair labor practices, maternity leave, and affordable childcare. Betty Friedan published the bestseller *The Feminine Mystique* (1963), which documented the dissatisfaction and disillusionment felt by American housewives attempting to fulfill the limiting role imposed on them by society. In 1966, the National Organization for Women (NOW) was founded by a group of feminists, including Betty Friedan. My friends and I joined the local chapter of NOW in Delaware, the League of Women's Voters, and the National Association of University Women.

My women friends and I became intimately involved in the women's struggle for equality in our state and became ardent feminists. We participated in the first Delaware Women's Conference, which was held at Delaware State College in 1977. The elected delegates were to represent the state in the first National Women's Conference, which was held in November of 1977 in Houston, Texas. Vicki Villalobos nominated me as a delegate, which started out as a joke, but to my surprise and chagrin, I was elected as the alternate delegate. Although I did not get the chance to attend the historic event, this symbolic act encouraged me to get more actively involved in the movement. We marched in front of Legislative Hall and stopped and cornered legislators to convince them to support the ERA. Rep. Bella Abzug visited Dover and gave legitimacy and support to our struggle to free ourselves from the tyranny of men and other conservative women, who did not want to disturb the status quo.

We were branded as unhappy "women's libbers" and "bra-burning feminists." I was called many names by my colleagues and acquaintances—the iron lady, the iron butterfly, member of the

National Association of Wenches. Some men and women in the community taught that our radical posture was fermented, in large measure, by our unhappy personal lives and that we were simply "dissatisfied housewives." Damn right! Who wants to be relegated to an inferior social role, where you're paid nothing to do laundry, wash dishes, cook, take care of the kids and pay the bills? To top it all, you're treated as if you left your brains in your previous existence and you absolutely do not get any respect. You are a second-class citizen in the greatest democracy in the world. Everywhere, men are free, but women are held in chains! Even my husband, Joe, felt uneasy with the new activism, which had personally affected his quiet life in small town Dover. I remember writing him a long letter, expounding on the economic value of a housewife.

In 1977, I decided to abandon the job of a housewife in favor of a full-time position as the director of Whatcoat Social Service Agency. A meaningful career actually transformed me into a better wife and mother. The boredom, the ennui of being a housewife, dissipated as my impoverished intellect was again engaged in the simple act of thinking and discussing topics other than laundry, diapers, and housecleaning.

In 1978, federal legislation was passed creating the Displaced Homemakers Program. When the State of Delaware advertised to fill the position of State Coordinator to set up the program, I was one of 120 individuals who applied for the position. I had to drive to Wilmington to be interviewed by Secretary of Labor Donald P. Whiteley. I went to the interview, dressed in my generic pantsuit and my stylish clogs and socks. I had a sleepless night before the interview and felt less than prepared to be drilled for this top job. Anyhow, I obviously performed better than I anticipated, because Secretary Whiteley offered me the job. In addition to this position, I had the good fortune of working in other leadership positions in the state of Delaware—responsible positions, such as executive assistant and legislative liaison to a cabinet secretary and deputy director within the Department of Labor. These high-level appointments provided me with the experience and opportunity to learn how to gain and keep power. By that time, I learned how to be politically savvy and discovered the seat of power in our small state, and I used my new-found knowledge to help other women and myself to move to positions of greater power and influence.

The How of the WomenPower Paradigm: Outlined below are the recommended steps that any aspiring woman can replicate to learn the foundational character traits and the suggested competencies discussed as components of the WomenPower Paradigm. The steps are simply an expansion and replication of the Plan Do Study Act (PDSA) technique that most of you are familiar with. It's important that you write down a plan that can serve as a guideline for action and improvement.

1. **Partner with a coach or a mentor and form an advisory team (Sisterhood Circle):** Web of influence
2. **Discover and define:** Needs assessment and data collection phase
3. **Draft a person-centered plan:** This is your strategic plan for power. Incubate and Percolate
4. **Act and practice**
5. **Assess and recalibrate:** Continuous improvement

Step 1: Partner with a coach or a mentor and form an advisory team (Sisterhood Circle): Have a mentor or work with a trained executive coach, depending on your aspirations and financial ability. In addition, it's doubly as effective to have an advisory team (Sisterhood Circle), which can provide you with expert guidance and advice on complex issues that might go beyond work-related concerns. Sometimes, women need the "wisdom of the crowd," the collective, to effectively problem-solve, to give and receive feedback, and to learn and master the culture of power. For example, as an executive coach, I have worked with several women leaders, who needed guidance and assistance in assessing their strengths and weaknesses. A handful of them have blind spots that have prevented them from seeing areas that need focus and attention. Sometimes, it's lack of self-awareness and inability to actively listen and reflect on what is being said. My role is to assist them in discovering areas of growth and becoming comfortable in speaking **truth** to power.

The coaching process is a collaborative, not an adversarial process, where the coach has to share negative information that the leader might not want to hear. There are occasions when it's difficult to develop skills and change habits because the leader fails to see the problem—for instance, a misalignment between vision and strategy and key performance goals, or repeatedly hiring incompetent and untrustworthy staff. I have worked with a leader who feels that she has great expertise in strategic planning, but who fails to see the clear misalignment between her vision of being the "top agency for individuals with behavioral problems" and her goal of expanding facilities to other states to promote the agency and increase revenues. Although it could be a worthy goal five to ten years later, at this moment in time, the organization has yet to deliver basic core services and excel in some of the signature programs in its primary headquarters. In essence, the leader I am coaching has been resisting my advice. So, what do I do? It's not my role to impose my advice on the leader, but rather to provide her with clear and practical reasons for my position and allow her to come up with appropriate solutions. Mary Beth O'Neill (*Executive Coaching*, 2000), author and executive coach, reminds us what the true essence of executive coaching is: "fundamentally, it is about learning **to be** with leaders as they navigate through their world, finding key moments when they are most open to learning."

According to a recent study published in the *Journal of Human Relations* (2018), when women seek mentors, they tend to look for someone who can be a friend rather than someone who can help them learn and grow. Roepe (2018) noted, "studies have shown women aren't getting the tough feedback they need to move ahead. The best mentors will push, dare, and confront mentees, and challenge them to take on projects they might otherwise avoid." In other words, it's best to get mentors who are not afraid to give mentees constructive criticism, and one who will provide them with a balanced view of their strengths and their weaknesses.

Consider membership and active involvement in a **Wider Network** of powerful women in your profession, in government, in the corporate world, and in the nonprofit world. Networking is discussed

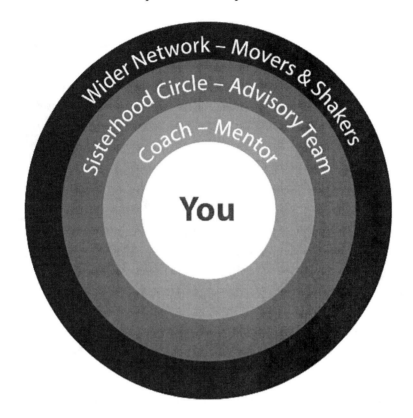

Figure 6: Circle of Influence—WomenPower Paradigm

in greater detail in the next chapter. **The Web of Influence** is graphically portrayed in the figure that follows. Having a mentor, a Sisterhood Circle, and getting involved in a Wider Network expand opportunities for growth, help you better navigate the complex problems faced by leaders, and provide you with a greater universe of support and advocacy.

Step 2: Discover and define: This is the needs assessment and data collection phase. What are the opportunities for growth and advancement as a powerful leader in your community? What are your needs, aspirations, and motivations? Define your statement of need and proposed solutions. It's also at this stage that you begin to scan the environment and **collect data**. Review, compare, observe trends. Benchmark the attributes of the powerful and influential discussed in this book (WomenPower Paradigm–Character & Competencies) with other tested frameworks. After much reflection and research, you're now ready to draft your plan.

As an emerging leader in the mid to late seventies, I did not have a woman mentor or a coach, or a network of supportive and knowledgeable women helping me navigate the untested waters of women in leadership roles. I also didn't have the foresight or the experience to face the battles that lay ahead. I was oblivious and simply didn't care about the resistance from men and other women because my husband had just died, and I was faced with greater challenges. I simply didn't know what I didn't know. So, I searched for role models like my mother; Dr. Rona Finkelstein, the director of the Delaware Humanities Forum; Karen Peterson, then a section chief for the Division of Industrial Affairs in the Delaware Department of Labor; and Senator Nancy Cook, a state senator for the 17th Senatorial District in Delaware. It wasn't until later in my early fifties that I learned how to penetrate the power structure in Delaware. My friend Paula Lehrer Shulak, who was then the chief clerk of the House of Representatives in Delaware, mentored me on the best strategies to understand and enter the inner sanctum of power in my home state. I did not have a written plan, although I thought about putting my thoughts in writing at some point in time. I was a wayward thinker and used untested strategies that worked most of the time. Paula's advice was invaluable in helping me achieve my career goals and gain legitimacy in state government and beyond.

Step 3: Draft a person-centered plan: This is your strategic plan for power. What is your mission and vision for undertaking this journey towards power? What's the end game, the unifying purpose? What are the objectives, measurable outcomes, and timelines for this critical endeavor? What strategies will you employ to achieve your strategic goals and objectives? These are the crucial questions that you need to respond to and reflect on. Let the ideas incubate and percolate before you start implementing the plan.

Step 4: Act and practice: To reap the benefits of a well-thought-out plan, you need to act on and implement your plan. Focus on the effectiveness of the strategies that you're using to achieve your objectives, the desired outcome, and the timelines. Do you need your coach or your Sisterhood Circle to help you navigate the unpredictable waters of the political scene, a domain that you're trying to penetrate? Do you have the stamina, the financial ability, the tenacity, and resilience to run for office? Is your plan in alignment with your key values and priorities? If you discover midway through the process that this power career track is not for you, try to regroup, modify your plan, and cut your losses.

Step 5: Assess and recalibrate: Since life and career are constantly changing, you might also need to assess and recalibrate your plan for power. I suggest that you review your plan every six months or annually, at the start of a new year, although it doesn't really matter when or how often you choose to review your plan. What's really important is that you have a recurring date and a designated frequency for the review and assessment. It has to be systematic, predictable, and not a hit-or-miss proposition. It cannot be a random act of improvement or else you might miss this critical step and not be as effective in reaching your goals.

CHAPTER 4

Remarkable Women and the New Power Model

IN MY INTERVIEWS WITH WOMEN profiled in this book, I noticed certain patterns of behavior that they have adopted and practiced that appear to have a positive influence on their ability to gain and keep power. The first one is networking and the second one is the ability to use an adaptive leadership style called situational leadership. In addition, the millennials interviewed appear to be comfortable with wielding and keeping power. The influence of this generational cohort in the power equilibrium is discussed in greater detail in Chapter 6: Let's Hear It from the Millennials.

The Collective: Networking

In an article published recently in *Time* magazine ("Three Queens to Rule Them All," 2018), Stephanie Zacharek describes the tumultuous and perilous journey that women attempting to lead and gain power have to experience and endure. "Sisterhood is powerful, but friendships between women can be among the thorniest flowers on earth. We often stand together, and need to do so for survival. But women, like all human beings, have flaws and frailties that sometimes tip into the red zone of defensiveness or distrust. Envy takes root like a weed; competitiveness becomes a blood sport...." Our friends and allies, other women, are at times also our worst enemies, in addition to the fierce battles that we sometimes have to face with men in power. How do we transcend the power struggles with other women and men? How do we build a strong and resilient coalition and galvanize others to support our mission? Alone, we could only force a crawling change in this intractable, systemic problem. It takes a ***collective, an alliance*** of strong and focused women to stand for their inalienable right to first-class citizenship and claim their universal right to govern their lives and their future.

Networking: According to a study recently published in the *Journal of Human Relations* (Greguletz, Diehl & Kreutzer, 2018), women build less effective networks than men, because women feel that it's not appropriate to use social ties to promote their careers. Most women engage in networking to develop support and friendship, not just to build business alliances. In comparison, men view networking as a form of work relationship, a business deal that is useful in advancing their careers, that could be ended when the relationship has served its purpose. Men use exclusive fraternities and societies to support and promote each other's careers and aspirations. The Skull and Bones Society at Yale University, founded by H. Russell in 1832, was apparently organized to tap the members of the power elite to run the government, business, and industry. According to an article published in *Business Insider* (McEnery, 2011), "rumor has it that Yale junior class members are tapped for membership each fall by some measure of leadership, influence and breeding." Membership in this exclusive secret society includes Presidents William Howard Taft, George Herbert Walker Bush, and George W. Bush; New York Governor William Averell Harriman; poet Archibald MacLeish; publisher Henry Luce; and conservative leader William F. Buckley, Jr., to name a few.

Women network through sororities, professional associations, church organizations, and other college or advocacy groups. However, there isn't a single powerful women's group whose sole unifying purpose is to groom women to be leaders of government, industry, and philanthropy. Perhaps, it's time that we follow the lead of men in this area. Be deliberate and systematic in acquiring power and be strategic in our advocacy efforts and fundraising in support of women.

Situational Leadership Style

A majority of our subjects appear to reflexively use the situational leadership model as their go-to style of choice. It is an adaptive leadership approach that allows leaders to be flexible and adjust their style according to the performance readiness and maturity of their employees, the needs and goals of their organizations and the external environment. Paul Hersey and Ken Blanchard pioneered this type of leadership concept, while working on their book *Management of Organizational Behavior* (1969). They classified leadership styles into four categories that describe patterns of behavior. The first style is *Directing*, where leaders tell their employees what to do because followers lack the specific skills to do the job effectively, although they might be motivated to do it. In comparison, in the *Delegating* style, leaders provide little guidance to employees because they have the desired skills and motivation to accomplish assigned tasks. In the *Coaching* style, individuals have some knowledge of the task, but lack the motivation needed to successfully do the task. Finally, in the *Supporting* style, followers have the required knowledge and ability, but lack the self-confidence needed to be effective.

When I was deputy director at the Delaware Department of Labor, I often used this approach in managing and leading my staff. However, I blended the two approaches (coaching and supporting) into a single category, which made it simpler for me to approach the complicated tasks of managing and leading. For example, Employee X expressed the sentiment that she didn't want to be "empowered" and wanted me to continue providing her with structure, directives, and guidance. It was in the late 1990s when "empowerment" was the buzzword in the workplace. She didn't want any of these novel approaches to working and managing, which simply confused and disoriented her and her fairly stable world. Employee Y, on the other hand, a highly-trained, curious, and creative individual, wanted complete freedom to shape her world. I delegated tasks to her and she simply checked in when the tasks were done. She flourished in this environment and carved out a new area of expertise in programming and grant writing. She brought in millions of dollars that allowed the agency to expand programs and services at a time when federal dollars were dwindling.

What's the best style of leadership? Hersey and Blanchard pointed out that there isn't a single approach to effective leadership and power retention. Success is better achieved through adaptability and flexibility and adjusting styles depending on the performance readiness and maturity levels of your employees, the organizational context, and the socio-economic environment. Companies such as Adobe, Anthem Blue Cross Blue Shield, British Telecom, the city of Battle Creek, Michigan, Genentech, the San Diego Padres, and the Royal New Zealand Navy have employed this model and outcomes have shown its effectiveness and staying power (Northouse, 2016). However, recent studies contend that despite widespread use of this approach by Fortune 500 companies, there is no empirical evidence nor data validating its effectiveness (Northouse, 2016; Thompson & Vecchio, 2009).

The Role Models

In the pages that follow, we will share with you the experiences of women who are successful in their fields and are recognized as outstanding leaders in their communities. A majority of the women we interviewed are from the East Coast and Southeastern regions of the United States, are between the ages of 40 and 65, and are leaders in public and governmental agencies, the health care industry, nonprofits, and small businesses.

Congresswoman Lisa Blunt Rochester: The Rising Star

I first met Lisa when she was appointed as cabinet secretary of the Delaware Department of Labor. She was in her mid-thirties and was the first African American to occupy this top-level position. She was energetic, approachable, and authentic. Her strength lies in her reflexive ability to connect with people by simply being herself.

She was endearing, charming, and low-key. She knew her strengths and weaknesses and selected the right people to work with her, not for her. Power and influence were simply part and parcel of her persona—she never demonstrated that she had a position of power; she simply connected with people, and they were drawn to her. It was the power of her personality that endeared her to people.

Before serving as the cabinet secretary for the Department of Labor, Lisa served as deputy secretary of the Department of Health and Social Services for the State of Delaware. However, it was as personnel director that she first made her mark in Delaware government. She was thrown into the limelight when she was asked to examine the allegations of racial discrimination within the Delaware State Police system. According to an article published by *Delaware Today* (Nagengast, 2017), "her report concluded that the agency was in technical compliance with the relevant laws but recommended numerous changes in policies and procedures to reduce the perception of bias." Her reputation as a consensus-builder, a collaborator, and a strong proponent of building positive bonds had its origin in this milestone event. Today, Lisa still wins over people with her message of tolerance, inclusion, and understanding.

The congresswoman exudes a rare combination of substance and skill, character and competency. During our interview, she acknowledged that self-awareness, self-knowledge, and knowing your values are critical to growing as a leader and a decision-maker. "Love is a stronger motivator than fear," she added, especially when attempting to influence the behavior of others. It's refreshing to hear a political figure express such acceptance and embrace of an aspirational model of truth. She noted that individuals need to look at the "whole truth," which at times feels like the objective truth, but truth at times resides on opposite ends of issues being discussed. She remarked that when considering complex issues like "immigration, criminal justice, mass incarceration, and good government," leaders have a moral obligation to consider "all perspectives" and hold a "dialogue with all relevant parties" to come up with an "objective truth." During this segment of the interview, her impassioned voice reflected her authentic commitment to the pursuit of the truth, which appears to be the antithesis of the current noxious political environment plaguing our nation's capital.

When our conversation shifted to the competencies that women need to develop to gain power and influence, the Congresswoman suggested that lifelong learning should be part of the competency model. She raised an excellent point that a cluster of knowledge-based and experienced-honed skills and abilities cannot be maintained at an optimum level without a continuing focus on learning and application. She agreed that the twin competencies of management and leadership are a "must-have" to be effective and successful. She reminded me that when she was cabinet secretary of the Delaware Department of Labor, she assumed the visionary and leadership role, while her assistant managed the day-to-day operations of the department. She added that there are many instances when "managers are not good leaders and vice-versa."

She felt that communication and people skills are critical to success. According to Bebe Coker, a family friend who has known Lisa since her youth, "building relationships, that's her strength." During the interview, she expressed her commitment to bipartisanship, that is, always reaching across the aisle to listen to the other person's point of view and to actively listen. She advised that when holding a conversation, "we need to be totally present; to be there and be accessible. Really experience 100% of wherever you are." I experienced this total immersion, this complete and unconditional focus on the moment during the interview. I could feel her immutable presence and focused attention on every word that I was saying, despite the fact that she had limited time to share with me and had to hop on a train to go to Washington, D.C., right after the interview. She explained that she had to participate in an important discussion in Congress. Her undivided attention, her ability to actively listen and focus on the moment, made me feel important; she made me feel valued.

The Congresswoman highlighted the importance of being able to solve problems and make decisions as skills that women need to nurture and develop. She pointed out that women need to be decisive, even when people make you question your decisions. She stressed that there's a need "to be decisive, since you can't make everybody happy. Seek the truth, do your due diligence, communicate with people and course-correct. Be inclusive when problem-solving so you can make a good decision." She also noted the importance of possessing political skills. She pointed out that "politics is not a bad word." We need to be politically savvy to "navigate strategically and to be able to communicate the message effectively."

Women can assist other women to be effective leaders by "advocating for each other, when in the room and when not in the room. We need to be there for each other." She added that "peer-to-peer mentoring is huge. I have a go-to friend when I am disappointed and when making difficult decisions." A behavior that she feels women need to drop is the propensity "to downplay their worth." It appears that despite "years of solid experience" in a field of endeavor, "women are still hard on themselves." She also would like to remind women that they have "choices." She recounted a time when she had two good job offers, but preferred the one with less pay. She developed a strategic plan of action, marched to the mayor's office, and asked for higher pay instead of accepting the initial offer. And she got what she asked for! Finally, she advised everyone to practice "self-care," since we're going through "tough and stressful times." She added that she is a "big believer in the use of professional counseling, meditation, and exercise, especially when making difficult decisions."

EARLY LIFE EXPERIENCES

In the United States, there is no traditional ritual, rite of passage or formalized training program for a president, his cabinet, members of congress or any national leadership position that could enhance their abilities to effectively lead the country. The royals go through a mentoring program on how to be a king or a queen and learn formal etiquette and ways of behaving as a member of the monarchy. For example, Prince William has been a monarch-in-training since his youth, preparing for the day when he will ascend to the throne, after his father, Prince Charles' reign. According to the *Daily Mail* (Greenhill, July 27, 2008), "his lessons in the Art of Kingship will include working in different Whitehall departments to get a better

idea of how government works, private instructions from consti-
tutional experts, and briefings by privy councillors such as former
prime minister Sir John Major."

To be a Dalai Lama involves getting training from primary
grades on not only in academic subjects but also on the Buddhist
philosophy. The 14th Dalai Lama's early training involved "the curriculum derived from the Nalanda Tradition, consisted of five major
and five minor subjects. The major subjects included logic, fine arts,
Sanskrit grammar and medicine, but the greatest emphasis was given
to Buddhist philosophy..." *(Birth to Exile: The 14th Dalai Lama,
Dalailama.com)*.

Although Congresswoman Lisa Blunt Rochester did not go
through a lengthy formal training program to be a congresswoman,
she worked in leadership positions in Delaware state government
and has been in public service for decades. Her father, Ted Blunt, was
a community activist, a city councilman, and an educator. He first
served as a Wilmington district councilman for 16 years and capped
his political career as the city council president for 8 years. Lisa
learned the art and practice of politics by watching her father, a successful politician, and by participating in his campaigns for reelec-
tion. Politics is in her blood—her younger sister Marla Blunt-Carter
served as an aide in Joe Biden's Senate office and was the state director for the Obama-Biden campaign. Marla also served on the White
House staff during the Obama-Biden administration. Because of the
family's active involvement in the Democratic Party, Lisa inherited
the support and endorsement of a powerful political machine—complete with a corps of supporters, powerful and influential decision
makers, and the flow of money and influence inherent in the system.

DISTINGUISHED EARLY CAREER

Lisa graduated from Farleigh Dickinson University, with a Bachelor's Degree in International Studies, when she was 23 years old. In
1988, she worked as an intern for Senator Thomas Carper, later as a
constituent relations caseworker. When Senator Carper became governor of the State of Delaware in 1992, she was appointed as the special assistant in charge of family issues. Less than a year later, when

she was barely 31 years old, she was promoted as deputy secretary of the Department of Health and Social Services, a responsible cabinet position within Delaware state government. Secretary Carmen Nazario offered the position to her twice before she finally accepted the offer. At that time, Lisa felt unprepared for the big challenge until Secretary Nazario convinced her that she had the ability and competency to succeed in the job. The secretary's reassurance and uncompromising belief in Lisa allayed her unfounded fears. At age 36, she became the youngest and the first woman of color to occupy the prestigious position of Delaware Secretary of Labor. At age 39, she capped her early career in Delaware government as personnel director of the Delaware Office of Management and Budget. At age 54, she was voted by the people of Delaware as the first female and first woman of color to become the United States Representative for Delaware's-At-Large Congressional District. For 227 years, the State of Delaware had only elected white males as congressional delegates, until the election of Congresswoman Lisa Blunt Rochester in 2016. This landmark event is even more remarkable, because Lisa is able to trace her ancestry and has proof that she was the descendant of a former slave through his voter registration card. During a fundraising rally in 2018, held at the Biggs Museum in Dover, Delaware, Lisa wore a scarf that depicted the image of her great-great-grandfather's voter registration card granted to him after the Reconstruction Era. He signed the card with an X because he could not read or write, but had to sign the card so he could exercise the right to vote. Lisa remarked that this is a reminder to everyone and an affirmation that even descendants of slaves can overcome any challenge and achieve their goals. What an amazing rise to fame, power, and leadership!

Servant Leadership

I have followed Lisa's career and ascension to positions of power and influence for more than two decades now. She has grown immensely, both personally and professionally, through years of experience, training, and commitment to serve others. The death of her beloved husband was a major turning point in her life, when she questioned her life's purpose and her place in the universe. It was two years after this tragic event that she decided to run for office. Her leadership style has developed and matured through the years, and, after years of practice, learning, and adapting, it has finally revealed its enigmatic face, value, and sparkle. Lisa aims to transform individuals and communities through servant leadership. It is a form of leadership that involves a delicate balance between being a leader and serving people. The phrase was coined by Robert K. Greenleaf in "The Servant as Leader," an essay that was published in 1970. Greenleaf explained that "the servant-leader is servant first.... It begins with the natural feeling that one wants to serve, to serve first. Then conscious choice brings one to aspire **to lead**. That person is sharply different from one who is leader first, perhaps because of the need to assuage an unusual power drive or to acquire material possessions...."

Lisa has typically led organizations with others in mind—whether it's standing for women on equal pay for equal work, making sure jobseekers are guaranteed livable wages, or affordable and accessible education that provides everyone the opportunity to realize their potential—Lisa is primarily focused on the growth and well-being of individuals and communities. She exemplifies the key qualities of a servant leader, such as putting the needs of others first and foremost, valuing the opinions of her employees and followers, developing other leaders, and cultivating a culture of trust. Lisa was never the command and control type of leader, rather she motivates and persuades people. She builds relationships, connects people, and finds common ground with individuals and groups who espouse opposite points of view. She is a consensus-builder and attempts to lead and change people's minds through inclusion, understanding, and compassion. She is not a disruptor who pushes to create change through radical ideas, audacious goals, and constant chaos. Rather she is the patient pioneer, the leader-in-waiting, who will triumph once the pendulum swings back to the middle. Lisa and leaders like her will carry the torch of leadership once chaos has created political change and a stable new system is ushered in. Leaders, with the competency and character of a public servant like Lisa, will be needed to maintain and sustain the long-term gains of the new social order.

Secretary Jennifer L. Cohan:
The Resilience and Tenacity of a Trailblazer

A Woman in a Male-Dominated Profession: Jennifer Cohan was sworn in as the 10th cabinet secretary of the Delaware Department of Transportation (DelDOT) on February 3, 2015, by then Governor Jack Markell. The agency was established in 1917 as the Delaware State Highway Department. It wasn't until 1993 that Ann P. Canby was appointed as the first female cabinet secretary of DelDOT by former Governor Thomas R. Carper. Secretary Cohan remarked during the interview that "she is a leader in a primarily male-dominated profession." Since 1917, only three female cabinet secretaries were appointed to head the department. At the federal level, the Department of Transportation, which was formed in 1966, has had only three prominent female leaders—Elizabeth Dole, who served from 1983 to 1987, Mary Peters, who served from 2006 to 2009, and Elaine Chao, who was appointed in 2017.

Although Secretary Cohan acknowledged that there are unique challenges to being a woman in a male-dominated position, she never used any of these impediments as an excuse for non-performance, special accommodations, or preferential treatment. She discussed her strategies on how she faced some of the typical problems of the department, without defensiveness, or accepting masculine cultural norms, or complaining about the lack of female role models in her profession. She simply shared some of the unique problems within her department and how she effectively and creatively solved them as a decision maker and a transformational leader. Early on, she realized that she has to fully engage and lead the workforce in changing the culture of the department through a well-defined selection process, where they "Hire for attitude and train for skill." She and her management team realized that not everyone is skilled at providing face-to-face customer service, so they hired consultants to map out the ideal process by using a technique known as value stream mapping (VSM). It is a lean management tool that uses a flow diagram documenting every step of the current state process from beginning to delivery of products or services to the customer. Waste and unnecessary steps are identified, analyzed, and eliminated before designing a streamlined future process (*American Society for Quality, Value Stream Mapping Tutorial—What Is VSM?* 2019). Jennifer remarked that with the implementation of VSM, employees were able to put themselves in the customers' shoes and realized their key role in delivering quality services. Appropriate training was also provided to frontline employees, who provide face-to-face customer service.

Relentless Focus on Customers: Secretary Cohan's relentless focus on customers, both internal and external, appears to be a winning strategy that's slowly changing the department's cultural landscape and improving its reputation as a department responsive to the needs of its citizens. She "walks the walk,";and she even could be seen visiting district toll booths and could be spotted with snow plow operators during wintry months. She has gained enough "street credit" for her people to accept her as an insider—one who is real, authentic, and relatable. She is a "Girl Boss" who is not afraid to take credit and promote herself when she or her staff deserve the credit, or to own mistakes, fix them, and then move on. She pointed out that DelDOTs job is a tough and challenging one—the public only sees the traffic jam because of ongoing construction in many work zones, but they fail to appreciate that all these temporary inconveniences and annoying traffic slow-downs are necessary to build and maintain good roads and a safe highway system. I personally feel that Delaware has one of the best maintained road and highway systems on the East Coast, especially compared with the roads and highways of neighboring states.

Let's Hear It from the Employees: To be a great leader, one needs to be able to give and receive feedback. Bill Gates of Microsoft reminds us that "we all need people who will give us feedback. That's how we improve." When I asked Secretary Cohan if I could interview her staff to inquire about her leadership skills, she responded with a decisive "of course!" There was not even a sliver of hesitation in her pleasant and friendly voice as she replied to my request. She recommended some names, and I asked for approval to interview others, which she confirmed with a decisive "yes!"

There was great consensus among the employees I interviewed that she is an outstanding leader because of her focus on customers and employees, her exceptional ability to communicate effectively and listen actively to the voices of customers, her use of data when making informed and quick decisions, and her subject matter expertise.

The pattern that emerged is the profile of a leader who knows who she is and is comfortable wielding the power inherent in her position and using it to benefit others. Employees repeatedly portrayed her as a great leader because of her focus on both customers and employees. Her powerful vision of providing the best customer service, according to one of her direct reports, guides her every action and decision. "Secretary Cohan empowers employees, builds them up, and provides them with the necessary resources, like training, to excel in their jobs," remarked one of the employees. Another appreciated her ability to motivate him "by giving praise, when praise is due" and concluded that their leader is a "great motivator." According to another employee, "she has this great ability to seek out talent and put people in positions that fit their competencies and interests." Employees are amazed at her ability to communicate effectively with all types of people and her success in navigating the treacherous waters of the political environment.

Not only is she able to communicate her vision to the funding agency, she is also knowledgeable about the budget process and has incrementally built powerful connections with decision makers. Within a six-month period, she was able to get the funding that other department leaders had attempted to get for many years. Finally, she is credited with changing the image of the Delaware Division of Motor Vehicles and the Department of Transportation, not only because she is admired and respected, but also because of her knowledge and competencies. She started from the bottom and moved up the ladder through hard work and outstanding performance. She worked at various state agencies—including the State Budget Office, the Division of Motor Fuel Tax and the Department of Natural Resources, and learned and harnessed her ability through training and experience. Because she is an expert in so many facets of state government, her people have great confidence and trust in her ability to manage and lead.

Stephen M.R. Covey (2006) states that trust is a hard-edged economic driver and a key factor in promoting success in the workplace. He explains that it's made up of two critical elements: one is character, which refers to an individual's intentions, integrity, and honesty. The second involves competence and results. When a leader is trusted by her employees, it results in an engaged and highly motivated workforce, accelerates and speeds up performance (when trust goes up, speed also goes up), and makes the organization efficient and profitable. It appears that Secretary Cohan's success can be attributed in part to the unflinching trust she has earned from her employees. This is a monumental achievement considering the size of the employee base, which is 3000+, and the diversity and complexity of the services provided by the department.

Rise from Rags to Fame and Power: Jennifer confides that she was born into a poor and dysfunctional family, with an alcoholic father who drank himself to death. College was never part of any conversation in their household, much less going to graduate school to get an MBA. She was literally a small-town girl, born in 1972 in Hartly, Delaware, west of the capital city of Dover, with a population of 74 according to 2017 Census data count. Taking cues and nourishment from the same murky environment, she followed the pattern and got married at 18 to another alcoholic. She had her daughter at 20 and divorced and became a single mom at age 22. The birth of her daughter was the critical turning point that changed her perspective and gave her a strong defining purpose in life. She worked hard and put herself through college while working for the state because she wanted her daughter to experience a better life.

Role Models and Gratitude: Jennifer started her long and illustrious career with the state when she was hired by Dale Shuirman, then director of the Division of Motor Fuel Tax. She was grateful to him for taking a chance on a young and inexperienced kid and for seeing the potential in her. Bob Voshell, former director of the Division of Motor Vehicles, also gave her the opportunity to succeed by hiring her for a full time and stable state job. Her big break came when former DelDOT cabinet Secretary Carolyn Wicks selected her as the first female director of the Division of Motor Vehicles. Before that appointment she served in a variety of leadership positions with the Office of the Controller General and the Department of Natural Resources and Environmental Control. How did a poor, small-town girl, from an impoverished social and economic background, rise to power in a politically-driven state government?

Character and Personal Traits: Secretary Cohan's spectacular rise from a deprived childhood to fame and power reads like a fairy tale, a fantasy of sorts. Like the protagonist in a novel, we look at her personality traits, the choices she made, and the people who supported her. Her mission of serving others—working to motivate and empower employees, focusing on customer needs and requirements, leading a department to improve transportation safety and commitment to community service—all point to a strength of character that's a categorical imperative for gaining and keeping power. Her lofty goal of promoting the common good is powered by her limitless and desirable traits, such as hard work, determination, infectious optimism, courage, and a sense of gratitude for her mentors and followers.

Bestselling author Brené Brown (*Dare to Lead,* 2018) states that having the courage to be "vulnerable" can transform the way we manage and lead in both our personal and professional lives. Jennifer is the quintessential model of a leader who is not afraid to embrace her vulnerabilities and imperfections. She embraces and owns her mistakes and her successes. She is not afraid of tough decisions and crucial conversations and "rumbles with vulnerabilities" with her employees and leadership team to identify problems and offer solutions. Her deep sense of authentic gratitude is inspiring. She credits her staff for all the innovations and improvements within her organization, gives them the glory and center stage when goals are achieved, and encourages them to excel and innovate. She engages and involves employees in implementing systemic changes to key business processes by eliminating duplication and waste through the "Enough Already Campaign," which encourages and rewards employees for identifying a process that does not add value to the final product or to the service delivery system.

Every October, the agency holds an "Innovation Fair," where employees compete and are rewarded for innovations that make their jobs easier and enhance productivity and satisfaction. For example, Mr. Mumbley, a snowplow operator at one of the local districts, designed and built a simple convex mirror for his equipment to enable him to see through the blind spots when clearing snow piles along roads. The leaders and employees celebrated his invention by having a pizza party and a town hall meeting at his local yard and videotaping the event. He was thrilled that his invention was viewed by thousands of people all over the United States, Africa, and the entire world.

When I asked Jennifer what behaviors leaders need to possess to keep power, she noted that they need to have "courage, consistency, and care." She added that courage means that "leaders need to talk up front, when things are good and when things are not so good." Consistency means "treating everyone the same way, whether you're talking to the governor or the janitor. You also need to listen, make eye contact, and be present when conversing with others." Care refers to her focus on employees and giving them the credit and the glory that they deserve. She is quick to give credit to her employees, her leadership team, her mentors, and her community partners. Gratitude appears to be a signature strength that guides her in every facet of her life, work, and community service.

Community Service: Americans are a generous bunch, both collectively and individually, not only in terms of giving monetary contributions but also in terms of volunteering their time to help those in need. This charitable behavior is extended not only to family and friends but also to total strangers. In 2016, the United States ranked second to the country of Myanmar in charitable giving, according to a report published by the Charities Aid Foundation (Davies, 2016). The total dollars donated by Americans to charitable causes was $373.25 billion in 2015. Jennifer, like the majority of Americans, is actively involved in giving back to her community and has a long list of organizations where she serves as a volunteer. What's different with her is her active involvement in causes that she believes in, which she considers part and parcel of her daily work schedule.

Volunteerism is not simply an extracurricular activity that she engages in when she has time; it's a critical part of her regular schedule. Her community engagements include serving as president of the Greater Dover Boys and Girls Club, chair of the Southern Delaware American Heart Association Board of Directors, and the Delmarva Council of the Boy Scouts of America. As president of the Greater Dover Boys and Girls Club, she forged a successful partnership with the Kent County government and launched a new joint-use facility at the Kent County Recreational Center. She also informally mentors women who are aspiring to move to leadership positions or further their careers and education. In addition to leading a major state department, she is also actively involved in professional organizations nationwide, such as the Association of State Highway Transportation Officials, The Northeast Corridor Commission, and the National Operations Center of Excellence, to name a few.

Passion and Inspiration—Teaching: When Secretary Cohan was interviewed for the Delaware Libraries Passion Project, she exclaimed that her passion is teaching. She is an adjunct faculty member at Wilmington University and teaches leadership and public policy at the graduate school. She is a lifelong learner and an information-junkie, who delights in her students' successes. In our taped interview, she marvels and is fascinated when a student finally gets the meaning of an idea that she's trying to convey, which she captures in these comments: "There's no bigger joy for me than watching my students when they actually get a concept and begin to understand it. It's literally like turning on a light bulb over their heads. It's a great thing to witness—the thrill of learning." Great leaders are great teachers and mentors. No wonder Jennifer is a success and by any standard, a remarkable woman of great power and influence.

Beth-Ann Ryan: Leading with Backbone and Heart

When I first met Beth-Ann, I knew intuitively that she would do great things. It was 2008 when she was first hired as an administrative librarian for the Delaware Division of Libraries. The division was implementing the Baldrige Criteria for Performance Excellence at that time, and the director asked me to introduce the concept to Beth-Ann. The Baldrige framework is a comprehensive system often used by business and governmental agencies to improve performance and implement innovations. She approached the task with excitement, determination, and confidence. I knew then as I know now that this gifted leader will go a long way. Sure enough, within a three-year period she was appointed deputy director for the entire division.

What her employees say: Beth-Ann responded with a confident "yes!" when I inquired if I could ask her direct reports about her leadership style. She is a confident and authentic leader, one who is easy to get along with and is totally approachable. Her direct reports and peers were in complete agreement about her signature strengths. They all felt that she is a great communicator—a leader who "knows how to talk and listen to employees from different generations," who actively listens to both sides of an issue and provides good advice, and is "good at putting things in perspective." They applauded her ability to promote teamwork, where collaboration is the norm. Her ability to resolve conflict, where everyone is a winner, is another competency that they valued in Beth-Ann. She's able to deal with difficult people and challenging situations by actively listening to both sides of the issue and by remaining fair and non-judgmental. Consequently, her employees felt heard and validated, and conflicts are resolved to everyone's satisfaction. They noted that they respect and appreciate her knowledge and competence in information technology and social media and expertise in diverse areas of the library system. Most of all, they expressed great respect and admiration at the way she handles power, where her focus is first and foremost the agency and its employees. She has never used power to benefit herself. She is universally admired, respected, and trusted by her employees not only for her knowledge and competence but also for her impeccable character and unique ability to balance work with fun.

Beth-Ann's signature strength is her leadership style, which can be aptly described as a form of *situational leadership.* She has a commanding knowledge of all her direct reports' personal and career aspirations, their needs, strengths, and expectations. She has a well-developed emotional intelligence and is adept at reading their facial expressions and listening to their voices, rather than silencing them. She is a *conversational entrepreneur,* one who listens with understanding and curiosity, frames the questions with clarity and compassion, and chooses the appropriate time to talk. She is present and confident and not afraid to face conflict, identify problems, and make tough decisions. She is positive, energetic, and expects the best from her staff, which creates trusting relationships and strong bonds that result in positive outcomes.

I first came across the phrase "backbone and heart" as an executive coach. I have read and have applied the concepts and practices introduced by Mary Beth O'Neill (2000) in her book *Executive Coaching with Backbone and Heart.* Beth-Ann's leadership style and her way of approaching power remind me of the "continual dance of balancing backbone and heart" as she manages and leads her staff, a team of consultants and other peers in the library system and beyond. Author O'Neill remarked that "backbone is about saying what your position is, whether it is popular or not. Heart is staying in relationship and reaching out even when the relationship is in conflict." I have witnessed Beth-Ann take a courageous stand on what she fiercely believes in, while actively listening and considering a point of view that's inimical to her stand. As she gently but firmly reminded me during the interview, "truth can be mean; temper truth with kindness. I can soft-pedal it without compromising my core values." There was an occasion when I was working as an organizational consultant for the division when she gently reminded me, in her positive and endearing way, to be more accommodating and patient since I accomplish tasks faster than most people. What a refreshing breath of fresh air! I have enjoyed and have learned from this young woman, who intuitively knows how to be a great leader and wields power with such magnificent mastery and infinite grace.

During all the interviews with the remarkable women profiled in this book, I asked them to assess the charts on Character Traits and

Suggested Competencies. Beth-Ann pointed out that I might consider including "personal traits" as part of the character piece. She noted that personal traits, such as self-confidence, flexibility, being collaborative, tenacity, and persistence are crucial in gaining and keeping power. For example, she added, "men appear to have greater self-confidence than women, or maybe they're better at faking it. Women are raised and taught to be quiet, to listen, to be polite, and not to take over meetings." We agreed that men are socialized to be self-assured and to lead, while women are raised to be sensitive to others and to be supportive rather than assertive.

Beth-Ann agreed that the eight core competencies listed in the chart are of critical importance. In terms of communication skills, she felt that listening without judging, communicating precisely and clearly, and avoiding vagueness are fundamental to effective communication. She remarked that problem solving and decision-making skills are two key areas that women "have trouble with" and are in need of additional training and practice. She further explained that women are afraid to make decisions, because it might prove to be the "wrong move" and oftentimes, "they do not know how to identify the root cause of the problem." Conflict resolution and political skills are two areas that she felt need attention among women leaders. She pointed out that competition is toxic and does not understand why women compete instead of supporting each other. She recognized the benefits of healthy competition, but cautioned women not to be threatened by the success of others. We agreed that there's enough of everything to go around—the success of other women does not diminish one's ability to succeed and wield power and influence.

She affirmed that political skill is important at every level, as well as building strong and resilient relationships and a deep understanding of the power structure within a system. Finally, she suggested that women need to be more collaborative and supportive of each other's career goals and aspirations. She remarked that in the majority, "women hoard information and knowledge, unlike men who support other men through active networking and partnership." A day later, she emailed me an article on why *"Women Build Less Effective Networks Than Men"* that was originally published in the *Journal of Human Relations* (November 14, 2018), which provided me with great information on the networking section in the previous chapter. Beth-Ann is a woman of great conviction and substance—a leader who models the foundational character traits and the competencies that we consider as desirable for anyone attempting to gain power and influence. I am certain that Beth-Ann is destined for greater and bigger things and will continue to transform the balance of power in our state.

Dr. Courtney Stewart:
Leading with Optimism, Grace, and Humility

I first met Deputy Secretary of State Courtney Stewart at a training event sponsored by the Delaware Quality Partnership for state employees and leaders. What impressed me the most about her were her sincerity, optimism, and down-to-earth attitude. She's unpretentious, modest, and wields power in a quiet but effective way. Power appears to be a reflexive and inborn aptitude that Courtney carries with her as part of her essence. She is respectful of authority and titles and refers to me, every time I bump into her, as "Dr. del Tufo." I didn't know until much later that she earned her doctor of business administration degree in 2012, when she was barely 30 years old and became a deputy secretary five years later. Her meteoric rise from a public utility analyst to deputy secretary (in six short years), in one of the key departments in the State of Delaware, is a monumental achievement. What accounts for her early success and her natural ability to exercise power effectively and instinctively?

Dr. Stewart was born in what can be described as a sepia-tinted, small-town Americana, named Selbyville, Delaware. It's a town with a population of 1,251 in 1980; in 2016, with the influx of Spanish-speaking immigrants, it expanded to 2,421. Until the late 1930s, it was the largest supplier of strawberries on the East Coast and home to Mountaire Farms, a poultry company that provided employment to the residents of the town. The Selbyville Public Library is housed in former U.S. Senator John G. Townsend's home, which is located at 11 Main Street. The senator's family donated his residence to the town after his death. Small town values, such as hard work, integrity, strong family ties, and community service have guided her throughout her youth and adult years.

Courtney remarked that her paternal grandmother, Anita, was a great source of inspiration and strength for her. She was a small business owner, who encouraged her to believe in herself and to have the confidence to pursue anything in life. Her parents and siblings were also supportive of her dreams and passions. Her subsequent move to Dover, the capital city of Delaware, where she completed a Bachelor's Degree in International Business at Wesley College, was a fairly uneventful move. Right after completing her undergraduate degree, she entered graduate school at the same college and completed an MBA. Two years later, she enrolled at Wilmington University in Dover, Delaware, to complete her doctoral degree. She has worked all her life in Dover, where after a little more than a decade, she has moved up the ladder of success to the number two post within the Delaware Department of State.

Millennial Influence: Courtney is a model millennial leader who demonstrates the best attributes of this demographic cohort, such as a focus on education, valuing diversity, ease and comfort working in a collaborative team environment, digital competence, and political savvy. She was well prepared when she entered the workforce and later as deputy secretary. Armed with a doctoral degree, solid experience in budgeting, financial management, legislation, and human resource management, solid and strong ties with the local power structure, and familiarity and comfort with the social and cultural environment of the capital city, Courtney's journey towards professional success was her only destiny.

Accepting Imperfections and Vulnerabilities: Courtney is well-aware of both her strengths and weaknesses and accepts things she is unable to change, but works on areas that she feels she is capable of improving. She is cool, collected, and open, even when sharing her vulnerabilities and areas of growth. She confided that public speaking is not one of her best skills, so she takes time to prepare every time she has to deliver a presentation or a speech before a crowd. Although she is an expert in many areas, like the state budgeting process, financial accounting system, and legislative process, there are subject areas where she seeks advice from other experts. She does her initial research, gets advice from knowledgeable staff or consultants, and asks questions to better formulate a solution or make an informed decision. She has an informal network of peers to whom she goes for advice and guidance. She is humble without being self-deprecating, knowledgeable without showing arrogance, and authentic, not only as a person but also as a leader. She fully embraces her vulnerabilities and finds perfection in imperfection.

Wabi-Sabi is a way of living that's focused on accepting the imperfections and transitory nature of life. It is a fundamentally Eastern way of thinking that is ingrained in the Japanese psyche. It is a worldview that accepts the temporal and imperfect essence of life and nature. It is also manifested in the Japanese concept of aesthetics in art, architecture, and poetry (del Tufo, 2015). It has its origins in the Buddhist teaching of the three marks of existence—impermanence, suffering, and emptiness (Leonard Koren, 1994). Robin Griggs Lawrence (2001) noted that "*wabi-sabi* reminds us that we are all transient beings on this planet—that our bodies, as well as the material world around us, are in the process of returning to dust. Nature's cycles of growth, decay, and erosion are embodied in frayed edges, rust, liver spots. Through *wabi-sabi*, we learn to embrace both the glory and the melancholy found in these marks of passing time."

How can we apply this uniquely Japanese value to improve the quality of our lives and the way we lead and handle power in our workplace? The knowledge that everything in life is temporary and imperfect makes us appreciate the gift of life and time with greater clarity and openness. Like Courtney, we might consider accepting things we cannot change and focus on areas where we're able to grow and learn. Like her, we can be authentic—embrace our vulnerabilities, our humanity, and valiantly improve critical areas of growth. As Lawrence aptly concluded, "...shift the balance from doing to being, to appreciating rather than perfecting." Like Courtney, let's discover perfection in imperfection.

Courtney's experience in the 21st century workplace was a far cry from the experience I had in the mid- to late 1970s. I was one of a handful of women administrators working for the Delaware Department of Labor at that time. I remember feeling uncomfortable when the men in the room started to question me as to why an inordinate amount of funds was designated for use by the Displaced Homemakers Program. The men chuckled at the term, and the budget director barked a question to the cabinet secretary, who then turned to me to respond to the question. With a hint of sarcasm, the budget director asked me, "what the heck is a displaced homemaker, anyhow?" In 1975, 43 percent of women (ages 25 to 34) were homemakers, while in 2016, only 14 percent were classified as such (*U.S. Census Bureau, Population Reports,* April 2017).

In 1978, federal legislation was passed creating the Displaced Homemakers Program, which Delaware promptly adopted. The Delaware Code noted that a "displaced homemaker is an individual who has worked in the home for a substantial number of years providing unpaid household services for family members; who is not gainfully employed; who has had, or would have, difficulty finding employment; and who has depended on the income of a family member and has lost that source of income or has depended on government assistance as the parent of dependent children, but who is no longer eligible for such assistance." A majority of the displaced homemakers who sought services at our centers were divorced, separated, or widowed. A significant number of men in the 1970s had a challenging time accepting women in the workplace not only as equals, but their mere presence as peers and leaders was enough to cause them consternation. To top it all, women felt similar sentiments toward other women entering the workforce or managing as leaders.

When I asked Courtney about the challenges that she might have encountered in the workplace, she paused for a long minute and could not come up with a single problem worth mentioning. She declared that all of her supervisors were very supportive, extremely smart, and knowledgeable and willing to explain anything or any task that was assigned to her. Although a majority of her supervisors were men, the women she worked with were also extremely supportive and helpful. She felt a kinship, a special sisterhood of sorts with the women working with her. The competition, the hoarding of knowledge and information, and the doubting posture of the earlier generations concerning women's ability to lead slowly have been erased by decades of legislative, cultural, economic, and social changes. Courtney's story has brought me a new-found optimism and renewed vigor that our earlier struggles were worthwhile, and we're now harvesting the initial bounty of a lifetime of work. We have women leaders who have come of age and are ready to take the plunge and change the world. ***Power, influence, managing, and leading are practices and rituals that are now part of the essential fabric of their lives.***

Rosemarie: Leading by Example

"Is this your idea of being here at 4:30?" the wife of the U.S. Embassy's *chargé d'affaires* roared. Twenty-two-year-old Rosemarie could only mutter, "I'm very sorry, ma'am," in reply. Faking confidence, Rosemarie, quick on her feet, decided against giving any explanations. She knew it would be misconstrued as making excuses. "But my knees were trembling for the first time ever in my life!" she exclaimed. "And I suddenly felt the urge to pass water right there at the gate of the diplomat's residence," she added.

It has been decades since that crucial catering event that she had to oversee occurred, yet the exchange remains seared in her psyche. The reprimand seemed stern for arriving 15 minutes late to deliver the food that would complete the buffet already set up since early that morning. After all, the cocktail party wasn't scheduled to commence until 6:00 p.m. But it was no ordinary party. The gathering officially welcomed the new U.S. Ambassador to the Philippines. Rose, as friends in college called her, had every reason to feel stressed from the pressure to perform well.

Rose's story began eight months earlier. Two weeks after graduating college with a science degree in Food and Nutrition, she started work as a "food checker." This rank and file position, intended to prevent pilferage, had become obsolete. Mobile devices virtually eliminated the job of matching order slips (receipts) with the prepared food that came out of the kitchen to dining room patrons.

"I was very disappointed on my first day of work. I thought to myself that after four years of college this was all I was going to do," Rose confessed. On top of that, like other food service schedules, the shift was on broken time: from 11:00 a.m. to 2:00 p.m. and from 5:00 p.m. to 9:00 p.m. Because she chose not to take a nap during the break, Rose went to the kitchen supervisor to ask for work to do, to observe and learn the process. After all, this was the United States Employees Association (USEA), the exclusive membership club of the diplomatic corps on U.S. Embassy property, with only the U.S. diplomatic mission as members. Rose did not despair, even if she would rather be training as a medical dietician.

Within the next eight months, however, a big fiasco occurred—the outbreak of what could have been food poisoning at the Marine Ball—which set in motion events that sealed Rose's fate. A U.S. team came to inspect the facility, which resulted in the temporary closing of the club's restaurant for cleaning and employee retraining. The brewing conflict between the food and beverage (FNB) manager and the club's general manager (GM) came to a head. The FNB manager went on leave, and the chief, who was responsible for the operations of all food service outlets, club, and private event functions, as well as the catering of U.S. Embassy parties, never returned. The kitchen supervisor under her also resigned. Only the banquet supervisor and captain waiters remained of the management team in-charge of all the club's food service.

In the chaos of departures and ensuing lawsuits, the club's general manager offered the FNB manager position to Rose after she had only worked there as food checker for a little over half a year. Out of deference to the departing FNB, who had recruited her and who was also close to her family, Rose declined this top job offer. She accepted the kitchen supervisor position instead. However, she performed the job of the FNB manager for the next three months, while the search for a permanent replacement was underway.

As acting FNB manager, Rose managed the food service operations and met with U.S. Embassy Consular staff to coordinate the catering events with them. She also had to oversee the welcome party for the new Ambassador at the *chargé d'affaire's* residence on the day road construction delayed her and the team's arrival for a quarter of an hour.

"Talk about being thrown into the open sea with no lifeline!" Rose quipped. "I had to learn the ropes under extreme pressure," she added. Rose also needed to prove that excellent scholastic achievement translated to success in the workplace, and that the GM made the offer for the FNB manager's position in earnest. She had just turned 22, straight out of college, with less than a year of experience.

"But I did it! I was able to get the cooperation, perhaps the sympathy, of everybody. They helped me get the top job done," Rosemarie proclaimed. The rest of her long career path took her to national leadership positions, overseeing the operations of international food brands for local family and big corporations. Each assignment followed the same trajectory. From handing over a turnkey food business to an investor-owner, back to again managing the food and beverage service at a five-star resort-hotel, even though she was not a trained hotelier. Her mantra remained the same: "study and learn-as-you-go and innovate to swim, not sink."

Power Defined: Rosemarie defines power as the ability to accomplish goals through people. "Power lies in influencing people to do what you want them to do to reach your common goals," she explained. Success is being able to achieve what goal has been set forth and in being happy with what has been achieved, not wanting for more. Setting clear goals prevents non-stop longing for success to happen, according to Rose. "Accomplishing goals need to be celebrated, exceeding them even more," she simply added.

Leadership Role and Being a Woman: "Being a leader is first of all showing a good example to your followers," Rose stated. "If followers cannot find anything worth emulating from you, you have failed as a leader. Because leadership is influencing people to do what you want them to, not by force or out of fear; the key is getting them to cooperate without much effort on your side. For that, followers have to believe that you are leading them to the right goal or the one you set with them." This can be done, according to Rose, if the leader has earned the respect of his or her followers, and they share a genuine leader-follower bond. For this bond or relationship to be healthy, team building is important. It is a crucial function and a critical leadership skill. Effective team building entails seeing each team member as equally important as every other member, no matter how small his or her role may be. Successful leadership and team building can turn weaknesses into strengths. A good leader knows how to turn disabilities into assets.

"I feel that this has nothing to do with being a woman. Women dominated leadership in food service operations, whereas men were more interested in finance and marketing. But now women have entered these fields too; everyone has an equal shot at leadership and positions of power regardless of gender. But first and foremost, a leader has to be respected, and must earn that respect from followers," she emphasized.

How is respect earned? According to Rose, every promotion to higher leadership positions created learning opportunities for her because of the challenges presented by new responsibilities and higher goals. She considered herself lucky to have three younger brothers, because growing up with boys made communicating with men and navigating male-female interactions a lot easier later. Based on both her career and personal life experience, she listed the following six requisites for leaders to earn the respect of their followers.

1. Integrity

"You cannot command or expect respect if you set a bad example to the team by not being compliant with industry or company quality standards and best practices yourself," Rose explained. In food service for example, the expiration date on ingredients is sacred and not merely information on the label. A manager at any level of leadership loses all respect if he or she instructs or allows the staff to change the expiration dates for his or her restaurant-outlet to pass inspection. Even if the manager did this only once, the staff would likely continue to amend other kinds of information even without the manager telling them to cheat. This is not only about the staff emulating a bad example, but the failure of leadership to impart the significance of compliance to standards. Cheating is about missed opportunities. None of the followers will have learned the difference between using fresh and expired ingredients and how that affects the business' bottom line. So why would they listen to other quality standard directives from management?

Rose also cited the temptation to relax or bend standards because a leader is beholden to a vendor for favors received. "Accepting gifts can compromise a decision maker's integrity," she said. Upper management's role may sometimes include double-checking the quality of bulk deliveries from vendors or suppliers. The dilemma is balancing the urgency to restock depleted supplies with the need to maintain standards. By rejecting deliveries that are sub-standard, the kitchen may not have enough to use. Integrity requires that standards be met. This is easier for any manager to maintain if he or she never once received free items as gifts from suppliers, no matter how insignificant those gifts appear to be. "If you accept that even once, it will be very difficult for you to call their attention to any breach, however minor," Rose remarked.

2. Honesty

As a leader, being truthful, not lying and not stealing go a long way, according to Rose. Controlling food cost by eliminating pilferage of food (both raw ingredients and cooked products) and cash is crucial to profitability. But the temptation to cheat can come to anyone at any level of power.

Take the case of managers' misuse of signing privileges to order meals from the menu of fast food or fast casual restaurants. Some managers, at any level, can knowingly or unknowingly abuse this privilege by instructing or allowing the cashier, crew, or wait staff not to enter the transaction in the register or Point of Sale (POS) device. Since a manager's bigger meal allowance is part of the remuneration/ benefits earned, the company's accounting system charges the cost of the food ordered to the Human Resources (HR) payroll account. In the meantime, the units of food or products that came out of the kitchen inventory are matched daily with the number of units of food recorded as sold at the POS. These numbers have to reconcile and discrepancies appear at the time of reckoning, even when erring managers think that one or a few lapses do not matter.

These types of dishonesty-by-omission appear seemingly harmless but can have cascading effects. The cashier or wait staff at the Point of Sale (POS) and the production team in the kitchen are both held responsible and accountable for controlling the units of food sold and food cost (or inventory). Based on experience handling several chain outlets, Rose mentioned that sadly, once pilferage at the management level begins, that particular outlet becomes "problematic." The whole management team loses credibility with the crew. Eventually, the staff is less motivated or less likely to follow other management directives or participate actively in programs to increase productivity.

Eventually, the problem outlet sticks out among the cluster of outlets in the area because total sales and profit goals are not met at higher regional, national, and management team levels. Unexplained rise in food cost is one of the most important metrics because it signifies profit loss. But worse, allegations of pilferage lead to finger pointing between the cashier (service crew) and the kitchen (production) staff, eroding the morale of the whole team.

Word of advice from Rose: Aside from knowing that companies install controls in the system to discourage dishonesty, mid-level managers should note that staff on the floor know the system, including the software, better than the managers because the staff at the point of sales use the POS devices throughout the day, every work day. "It does not pay to be a dishonest leader when your followers are likely to know more than you do how to cheat the system," she noted.

3. Sincerity

"Mean what you say, and be the example," Rose simply stated. "If you remind the team of what they should do, make sure you comply by doing the same. For example, if you tell your team that they should be on time for a general meeting scheduled outside regular hours, then you should be there on time, if not earlier, even if you are not presiding. It sounds like a joke if you call out your managers for not starting their meetings on time, if you're not there yourself."

"Your followers will know how good a leader you are by your sincerity," emphasized Rose. It means, according to her, that if sanctions were prescribed for acts of non-compliance, the leader needs to impose sanctions following company procedures. "Otherwise, no one on the team will likely walk the straight path with you, the leader," she explained. Those led will think that their actions of non-compliance, like the leader's words, are inconsequential. "This is, by the way, founded on conditioning as we've learned in Psychology 101," Rose added. "This is also why you, as the leader, must follow rules and regulations stipulated by the company HR. Otherwise, you cannot command following or respect if you are not a good follower yourself."

Another meaning of sincerity in the workplace, according to Rose, is being honest about performance evaluation. The team should know that "Good Job!" means work done well or up to company standards. Everyone can detect insincere flattery dispensed to further one's interest, rather than to offer authentic assessment. "Especially when talking to employees one-on-one, be honest; everyone can quickly sense or 'feel' when you are lying," Rose emphasized.

4. Knowing what is right and wrong

"It would be impossible to give anyone what you do not own or teach knowledge that you do not possess. If you want your team to have a clear sense of right and wrong, then you, as the leader, should not only know the difference by heart, but also live it accordingly. Integrity, honesty, and sincerity will allow you to consistently demonstrate that 'right is right' and 'wrong is wrong' by example," Rose explained.

Rose gave her refusal to sign padded invoices from a pest control company as the best example of this. Due to the chaos of peak service hours and a high-energy work atmosphere during set-up and preparation time, it is easy for hands-on managers to quickly go through the day's paperwork and sign requests for payments without reading details. This was the case with a set of invoices, pre-dated for the previous three months for a pest control service, which Rose did not personally see the vendor come to deliver. Her refusal meant the provider was not going to be paid for what he claimed he provided, and it led to a lawsuit. Rose left the final decision to the hotel-resort owner. But she stood her ground, because had she buckled down and signed, the message to the rest of the staff would have been that truth or verifiable facts, like dates or attendance, could be manipulated to suit a specific end.

In the food service industry, pilferage is the number one activity to watch closely because the resulting losses could cause the business to collapse because profit margins are narrower. As such, zero tolerance on pilferage is an industry standard. But pilferage of supplies, raw ingredients, or cooked food products can be difficult to monitor. Food can be consumed or stashed away. The delivery of supplies can be another opportunity or source of temptation to engage in shady activities for short-term gains. One example would be the restaurant manager who over-reported the number of goods or units delivered (e.g., six sacks), versus the actual number or amount received (e.g., four sacks). He then pocketed payment for the difference, in collusion with the vendor. Because most or the majority of the team, including the stock man, the receiving cashier, and all other managers understood clearly that dishonesty and theft were wrong, two people came forward together to report the manager's behavior to higher management and personally to Rose. It helped that the two knew that pilferage was not to be tolerated. They were also aware that Rose would implement the zero-tolerance rule. Knowledge that the erring manager would be terminated empowered the whistleblowers because they understood that retaliation would not be a possibility.

5. Being respectable

Rose explained that while it is important to pay attention to physical appearance, it is even more important to manage how a leader is perceived. "How you carry yourself and your manners should signal respectability. A healthy bond or a successful relationship between the leader and follower is only possible after mutual respect has been established," she commented. Actions and language should therefore align with how one leads, which means leading with integrity, honesty, and sincerity.

Rose revealed that the late Margaret Thatcher served as her role model. She had several other women role models like her first food and beverage (FNB) manager at the U.S. Embassy club and the extremely detail-oriented area manager when she started in the international fast food chain business. But Thatcher's firm, even stern, stance and appearance appealed to Rose, who admitted that copying Thatcher came in handy as she plunged head-first into new leadership roles to address problematic situations or dysfunctional teams. For example, Rose was specifically assigned to oversee an outlet where the manager was perceived as "one of the boys" by the crew. The blurring of professional boundary lines between leader and follower had shifted relationships too far to one extreme. Business goals were not being met, because the leader had lost respectability. The manager's authority was compromised because followers failed to respond to her leadership role; instead they acted as though their leader was just a regular friend.

Rose cautioned that maintaining "respectability" both as a person and leader does not mean being harsh or abrasive. "Always be cheerful and pleasant at work," she said. "Also, as soon as you arrive at the workplace, all personal issues, including family problems, should be put on pause," she concluded. "It is good for you, your career, and your health; the short break from thinking of your personal concerns during work hours can be therapeutic."

More importantly, however, this is why developing people skills is crucial to leadership, according to Rose. She said that it is critical to remember that co-workers are people; they are not inanimate objects or robots that will move, respond, talk, or follow commands at the push of a button. "You should know how to handle people with emotional intelligence," Rose remarked. "This is where flexibility comes in handy; you cannot be too rigid. You should learn as much as you can about people. And you definitely have to adapt your interpersonal communication and management styles with the changing times."

"I can compare the attitude of staff from over several decades ago with what I have to deal with these days, and it is like night and day," Rose observed. "The 18 to early 20s crew of the 80s and 90s in the fast food and fast casual restaurants were more likely to follow instructions and standards on what needed to be done, with no questions asked. Back then, you would hardly hear them say, 'No, this is what I want to do,' because it was easy for them to understand the standards and the rationale for having high standards. They were more serious about what they did because they considered their fast food job as a means to an end—the proverbial stepping-stone to their future. As proof, I have seen them reach top-level management positions in the food industry now, and I cannot be any prouder of them."

"Staff from the 2010s practice a different work ethic. They seem to be attuned to hard physical labor, which eight hours of food service can be. They also appear less serious about what they do for work, as if working is just to pass time, or something to do because peers are doing the same. However, while previous batches of 18-year-olds were a bit timid, the present generation is more confident and self-assured. Previous generations intuitively understood the authority of position; younger ones take longer (if at all) to understand the value of work experience that elders bring to the table. I have learned to expect behaviors to change as generations transition," Rose reported.

"What worked for me was to befriend them, but only after establishing mutual respect and boundaries. I show interest and try to know who they are and the life they live," Rose explained. Because new entrants to the workforce or different types and cohorts of employees may be unaware of boundaries, they unknowingly test limits. They need to be told or shown these boundaries. According to Rose, this is where the job of the leader is to lead by example, strictly following and implementing company rules at all times. For example, in the resort-hotel industry where employees needed to be shuttled to the work site, arriving late at the pick-up station meant being unable to get to work (food service duty) on time. One morning at the 6:00 a.m. start of the breakfast buffet, Rose realized that three servers were missing. So, when they arrived an hour later, she sent them home even though she knew she had to bite the bullet and be even more short-handed for a fully-booked lunch service. Despite being on "friendly terms" with employees, Rose said that she had to demonstrate strict adherence to company policies on tardiness for it not to ever happen again. No one came late again after this incident, according to her.

Rose mentioned that she would accept invitations and attend social events important to co-workers. She laughed and joked with them. She knew never to reprimand anyone in public in the middle of service or use certain language with specific groups. But she made sure everyone knew that adherence to company rules and standards came first, and that compliance sets the limit.

6. Being a lifelong learner

"Be five steps ahead of everybody, so you lead and everybody follows. How? STUDY, STUDY, STUDY and READ, READ, READ. Pay attention to what trainers and mentors recommend for you to read, even if it is outside of your area of expertise or interest. Go for it," Rose advised. Further, she noted that "Knowledge is a requisite to effective leadership, and to a successful life. The number one skill to have is constant self-improvement. Knowledge does not come from a college or graduate education alone, but from countless training opportunities. Ultimately, it is how you implement this knowledge that determines success. Once you have studied the principles and best practices, it falls on your creativity to adopt and adapt them to what would work for each scenario."

Rose remarked that "Innovation is key. Back in the 90s, before emoticons, in order to make 18 and 19-year-olds remember to complete the late-night cleaning and closing protocols as well as to remind them to follow company standards, I created the 'YEY and the OOPS' board in the back office. Adapting a newspaper article concept, I drew two columns next to the crew's names on the board. One, the YEY column, was to praise them for anything they did well and the other, the OOPS column, was to remind them of any tasks they missed. Next to their names, I would put a cut out of a star if they did a good job and a sad face paper cut out if they forgot to do something. It was a hit because the teens thought it was fun. The 18-year-olds were excited to see who got a plus or minus. Adapting popular quiz game formats can be a great way to motivate employees to memorize rules and company standards, which can sometimes become meaningless and boring to them."

"These days it is easier to innovate; the Internet is a library at your fingertips. Doing research has never been faster, and information has become borderless. Know, experiment, and apply the best methodology to accomplish your goals to suit your target age. Think of something fun for the crew to do at every phase, but be mindful that this idea of fun and games could change over time. For instance, present generations are relatively more receptive to visual stimulation, whereas the 90s generation tend to enjoy experiential learning more. The games or fun learning activities that you pick should change," Rose cautioned.

"But even when you are not dealing with motivating personnel, you have to be innovative. Always ask yourself, 'How can I improve this situation?' In the fast food or fast casual dining business, one part of the report would ask, 'What have you done that's new for the month?' This question forces you to innovate, do what has not been done before. Everything constantly needs updating. Pay attention to competitive updates or answer the question, 'What has the competition done lately?' You have to read!" Rose concluded.

When Rosemarie declined the top position to manage the food and beverage (FNB) service operations eight months after she was hired as a food checker, she took the challenge to do the job anyway. Back in those days, she said that training employees for a job was not the norm or standard practice. "So it was up to you to learn everything by yourself. You have to analyze how systems work, and if there is something you don't understand, you find the right person to ask. No one will volunteer to help or train you," she recalled. Today, those aiming to reach positions of power and leadership, of all genders, have pioneers to thank for the trails that have been carved out for them. But following in the pioneers' footsteps means exactly that. Leaders with followers blaze open new paths through tenacity, hard work, and relentless innovation.

The Towering Wisdom and Solid Experience of Christie Nolan

Christie Nolan is an organizational consultant with rich experience and a wealth of knowledge in coaching and mentoring women leaders and assisting organizations thrive, grow, and innovate. In this section, George Banez, my guest author, and I agreed to present the interview in the first-person narrative to give the reader a sense of immediacy, a feeling of actually being there and listening to the perspective of this subject expert, rather than hearing the writers' point of view. We hope that the reader can hear her voice, feel her presence, and profit from her expertise—undiluted by our perceptions and personal perspectives. Here's Christie, in her own words. Let's pause and listen to her voice.

Understanding That Power Is Dynamic: Power is the ability to influence others, or others' behavior. When I hear the word "power" there is almost an aversion to it. But from my experience, power is dynamic. Something can be said for the subtlety of influence. I find that influencing change even from behind the scenes, for an introvert like me, can be incredibly powerful. I don't necessarily have to be the CEO or the Chairman of the Board in order to exercise power. The challenge for me is to be creative in the tools I use and develop to guide and facilitate change. Often, people who try to hit a nail with a screwdriver are not as effective. I also believe that "cleverness" is not in being just the hammer, but in the skillful approach to influence end results.

Negative associations with the "power" terminology come from what I call "inauthentic" power, or power by virtue of position or money. It is not necessarily earned. "Authentic" power on the other hand is the power that others are willing to give, because they want to follow a leader, one who inspires them and whom they respect— someone with integrity or character attributes that they admire.

I also prefer "power with" rather than "power over" others. We know from experience that when power is shared that results in collective power or leadership, better and faster decisions are made. A diverse group, or one more inclusive of women and minorities—those who have not been part of positions of power—promote strong ownership of decisions made, resulting in more positive outcomes.

As for myself, power is really about influencing change in the community that I've come to love. I see the nonprofit sector as a significant partner in creating community change and improving people's lives. Helping others claim their power and make the best decisions is a big part of what I do professionally. I work a lot with groups and group dynamics to facilitate group discussions to ensure that all voices are heard.

Approaching power (influence) from a place of wanting to do what's good, and not just for selfish reasons, motivates me. In my mind, this worthwhile pursuit makes me truly successful. It's not about money. But rather, it's the feeling that I have made a significant contribution in my lifetime. When all is said and done, when I look back, it is about what I am able to say I have accomplished.

What Is Success to Me? Success is the peace of mind that comes with having the freedom to choose. The longevity of being self-employed for the past 11 years in itself could be my definition of success. But it is also the freedom to create balance that allows me to pursue professionally what gives meaning and value to my life. This career choice capitalizes on my natural strengths and skills while giving me time to do what feeds my soul as a well-rounded human being. I made an intentional series of choices in my life that have led me to the place where I am right now—a beautiful place to be. I'm very content, professionally and personally.

Education: So much of who we become is shaped in our early years by our parents, and the circumstances we were born into. These too heavily influenced the path that I took in my professional life. First in my family to go to college, I earned a Bachelor's Degree in Psychology. I then went on to graduate school because I was told that just an undergraduate degree was not enough. During my last year in college, I learned of a course of study that really appealed to me, industrial organizational psychology, which is about applying the principles of psychology to the workplace.

I had been working since I was 12 years old. So, in my young mind, I thought I would be working until I was probably 65 to 70 years old or older. The idea of being able to improve the work environment for others to have a more productive and successful experience attracted me to the field. We spend a lot of our lifetime working! Industrial psychology led me to a career path in the non-profit sector, but the roots of that really originated in my childhood.

We grew up with not very much. My parents were teenagers when they had me. A single mother essentially raised me. Nonprofit organizations were there to be helpful when we needed extra assistance. A career in this sector really felt like a personal way for me to contribute in a meaningful way to help nonprofits be even more impactful and successful in accomplishing their missions.

More than anything, sometimes we get a lot of mentorship in a reverse sense of what we don't want to be. Within the family dynamics I grew up in, there were lots of examples of what not to be.

I knew education was the clear path out of that cycle. I love to learn, and so I was very good at school. I read voraciously. A lot of the books I read as a young girl had very strong, creative, and smart young women in them. They in turn strongly influenced me. If I would say anything, education is central. You may not get experience through formal education, but it lays the foundation for all future learning. It allows us to be reflective in thinking, taking in new information, processing that knowledge, and applying it as we evolve.

Early Start: Mom as Boss and Model: My mom came from a long line of entrepreneurs. She started a business of her own cleaning new construction homes and office buildings. She was and still is one of the hardest working people I've ever known. She's the roll-up-your-sleeves, "let's get in there and do it" kind of person. She's not one you'd see just sitting around. My work ethic really came from growing up with that example.

Mom had me when she was 16. But she went back to school and got her high school diploma. For many years, she went to work every day as a dental assistant. But that wasn't for her. Seeing her as an entrepreneur, as a role model, helped me recognize that I don't have to work for somebody else or be part of a system to be successful.

I started to work with her in the evenings and on weekends.

Yes, at age 12, I would rather have been doing fun things with my friends instead of cleaning bathrooms and offices with my mother. But this work made me humble, and it gave me a sense of purpose for my future. Knowing that this was not something I wanted for my life, because I wanted something greater, I made choices that led me to what I define as a successful life. More than anything, it gave me the resilience and the commitment to stay in school and do well. Even through college, I continued to clean offices on my own. I also worked as a legal assistant for a law firm, and I went to school full time.

I found very early in my career that I was a bit challenged working for male bosses, or anybody whose leadership style was "command and control." That really did not work for me. Being fiercely independent influenced my choices. Having somebody tell me what to do in an authoritarian way did not bring out the best in me. I recognized early on that this environment was not conducive to what made me thrive.

When the opportunity presented itself, or I should say, when I created the opportunity for me to go into business for myself, I really didn't look back. I knew that I was setting the stage for my future at that moment. It was very scary. I sensed that it was going to be a challenge. But I also knew I had some entrepreneurial history and some models to follow. I gave my business the best that I had because that was what I wanted for my life—the independence that came with being my own boss.

"What, are you stupid?" Thinking ahead in my position as vice president at the Community Foundation (Sarasota), I knew what my career path would look like. I had the opportunity to interact with a number of consultants who were doing the work I thought I would want to do some day. That was helpful. But as always, very poignant moments, like triggers, set me on that path quicker than anticipated.

One early morning, we were getting some things ready for a meeting. My boss at the time stopped in his tracks in the middle of a conversation and looked at me. "What? Are you stupid?" he said. I was caught off guard because nobody had ever talked to me quite like that, especially not in a professional setting. I said, "Excuse me?" I wasn't just going to take that comment. To me personally, one of the worst things anyone could do is say something so demeaning like that. In that moment, it was as though my boss didn't even think about what came out of his mouth. Right there, I lost all respect that I had for this man. I could never work for him in good conscience anymore, because he didn't respect me. He didn't speak to me with respect. I decided that it was the time to set the process in motion for me to become independent.

Going National: I didn't want to leave the Sarasota community. But I took a great opportunity to move to Washington, D.C., which is the hub of the non-profit sector in the country. I knew starting a new business would be a challenge in a new community, but if I were to be successful, in my mind, D.C. was the place to go.

I remained very intentional and thoughtful about my plans. Being deliberate in the transition, I started to make a lot of connections up in D.C. I made a lot of trips before the move, and before I arrived, I had my first client, which was the Community Foundation for the National Capital Region and now the Greater Washington Community Foundation. They ended up being my client for the first six years of my consultancy business. Eleven years later, I'm back in Sarasota and I have everything that I want. I am happy to have enough clients to keep me very busy here.

Two years of Washington, D.C., was a wonderful experience. I wanted to experience living in a big city. Being at the nexus of the nonprofit sector excited me. But since I grew up in the country, I needed land and space. I love Sarasota on so many levels, and the D.C. weather wasn't conducive to the life I wanted. So, I decided to move back to Sarasota, but continued to travel back and forth to D.C. for clients for a number of years.

D.C. helped shape me and my business in its the formative years. But the takeaway from D.C. for me was the beauty of diversity and inclusion in that geographic area. It really helped me, being from Indiana, to broaden my diversity lens. It influenced me as a leader in the work I do now with nonprofits.

On Being a Woman Leader: Emotional Intelligence (EQ) is the foundation for everything, including power. In order to be powerful, one needs to have a high level of EQ. I break down EQ into: (1) self-awareness and self-management, and (2) relationship awareness and relationship management. The ability to reflect on who we are, being self-aware or understanding of others' perception of us—be it as woman, minority, or somebody young—can be a valuable competency to have when discerning how to approach a situation.

As women, we certainly have to be aware of how we are perceived in general. We have to understand, historically, where we come from as a country and how women here had been treated as property. Similar to slaves with masters, women were subjects to their husbands. We recognize that power was automatically given to a man, whereas women have to work hard to earn it.

Being self-aware (knowing who we are and how we are perceived), while having the ability to read situations, allows us to be flexible and nimble. By understanding the dynamics of what is going on, it is easier to be adaptive. Knowing what a situation calls for helps guide our choice of tools to use, say for example, in bringing a group to an end result from point A to point B. Creativity also becomes necessary in influencing outcomes.

Awareness of other's impression of us is important. People make up their minds very quickly based on appearance. For example, women who are considered attractive are oftentimes received more openly by those in powerful positions. Men, in particular, are prone to listen more readily. We have to know that first impressions influence how others respond to us.

The brain is wired to make very rapid judgments even when information on hand is incomplete. Often, judgment is formed based on past experience, real or perceived, prior to a person knowing the facts. Aside from appearance, how we carry ourselves with confidence and how well we communicate determine whether others give us power, and whether they are open to hearing what we have to say. I will talk more about communication below.

Relationship Building, Trust, and Authenticity: I developed the ability to quickly read people and situations at a very young age. I also had a sense or strong moral compass of what is right and wrong early on. Both are key to people skills. I believe that gaining power is all about relationship building, because we can't really achieve or do anything without others. We all want to be part of something that is bigger than any one of us can do alone. We connect with people, build bridges, and nurture relationships ,because it is in partnership that we are able to create change.

How can we use power to influence others, invite them to come along for the ride and be part of a solution or a vision of what success looks like that is held by all, and not just by one person? TRUST. Others are willing to give power to the one with integrity, someone they trust. In the workplace, once competencies have been established, the question is whether a person can be trusted.

I listen very well. To be an effective communicator and for people to open up to me, they need to trust me. Both my coaching and organizational clients disclose a lot of very personal information to me. For me to be successful in the work that I do, people need to know that they can trust me. That is absolutely sacred. I would never compromise that trust. If I don't have that foundation, nothing can be built on top.

I also add to this AUTHENTICITY. Being real or not pretending to be someone else and being honest, or to be comfortable in our own skin, carry us beyond our self-interest. When we come from an authentic place in connecting with others, relationships are authentic as well, not superficial. One way to authenticity is being ok with being vulnerable. Vulnerability is about our willingness to be wrong and acknowledging mistakes. In a group, the person in a position of power who is always right, unwilling to ask questions, and has all the answers will have no followers. We know that no one can have all the correct answers all the time.

As a lifelong learner, I have always read books to evolve and grow. But I also do self-work to look at patterns of behavior in my life. Then I begin to understand my insecurities and my blind spots. Now I read to be even more helpful to others in their work on themselves. As a leader, I'm always asking the question, whether to an individual or organization, what they need and how I can add value to them. I listen. Then I let them know what they get when they spend time and work with me, instead of the other way around. That's because I want the relationship to be authentic.

I listen.... I speak up. In my experience, women are much more sensitive about what they say and how it might affect the other person. There's a lot to be said in the way that we, women, were raised. Messages that we received from our first family shaped and informed us about politeness, gender, and power. As women we want to be liked, as all people do, and being polite is part of it. But sometimes we have to say and do that which may not be popular or make us everyone's favorite. Most are unwilling to risk being liked to do what is right.

Growing up I also understood that some topics were "unspeakable"—particularly those that made adults uncomfortable. We don't necessarily put a spotlight on those who stand out, and the familiar becomes part of our norms in the society; we go through the motions of acceptance with no questions asked.

I was intentional in developing skills to become comfortable in shedding light on a situation or always presenting a different perspective. The coaching I received helped me develop those skills, because power comes from revisiting the un-discussed. Regardless of our gender and upbringing, we owe it to ourselves to speak up, especially when we see something happening. As I reflect, those moments that I didn't speak up were moments of regret. And they bring unpleasant feelings. I made a commitment to myself not to have regrets for not speaking up. I no longer hold back when compelled to speak my truth despite all the messages to the contrary growing up.

There Is Power in Your Voice: Speak Your Truth: In meetings, I see a lot of women unable to have a voice, or not have enough courage to speak their truth for fear of being wrong, judged, or offending someone. I notice this quite a bit, and I call it "polite dysfunction." Women don't have the opportunity to get a word in, because some older men have the tendency to dominate the conversation. Women may not be as assertive because of the way we were raised, and others may consider it disrespectful to interrupt.

Older men who have held positions of power are much more

likely to speak up without necessarily thinking of consequences. Even younger men who have not had power may not say much, which makes it more of an age rather than a gender issue. Introverts are also likely to stay quiet. Regardless of gender, however, across the board, the power dynamics within a group can influence someone's willingness to speak up. In group settings, people don't talk because they oftentimes sense that what they say is not going to make a difference. They ask, "why should I put myself in a position to be attacked or be vulnerable if I don't even have power to exercise?" It is important to recognize and overcome these barriers and learn to speak up.

Avoid Gossip; Instead Let's Bring Each Other Up: I was having lunch with a young woman who mentioned that another woman at a nearby table didn't negotiate as much as she could have gotten when she was promoted to a big CEO position in the community. Although my associate had insider information about the other woman's compensation package, I thought it was very inappropriate for her to disclose private information about someone I didn't even know, because gossip could shape my perception of that person.

At that moment my heart went out to the other woman, because I can empathize. How many times did I try to negotiate a higher salary with a man and found it incredibly challenging to ask what I felt I was worth, getting pushed back and finally giving up! It was just easier to keep the peace by not making a comment, and because I didn't want to be difficult.

I was just starting to cultivate a business relationship with my lunch partner, but if I'm interacting with somebody who is talking about other people or uses negative language, then I don't want to spend very much time with her, or not more than I have to. Here is a woman saying that another woman was taken advantage of. The advice I would give to women is not to engage in this type of negative behavior. I would say instead, to build people up regardless of gender. Never negate other people with gossip; instead be positive, because words give us energy. Be somebody whom others seek out and want to be around.

Strengths and Weakness: According to the *Gallup 2.0 StrengthsFinder*, of my top five strengths, four fall in the category of strategy. I have pursued strategic thinking and planning as a service to my clients, because I do it well. I love it, and it comes naturally to me. When I get into the flow, I don't necessarily have to sell myself. I talk about what it is I provide, and they see my passion. Once competencies and trust are established, then it is about passion, because we all want to be inspired.

People see me as a change agent. Clients want to create something different than what they have, and they just cannot necessarily navigate transitions on their own. I see my role as a Sherpa guide to help them look out for challenges ahead, mitigate risks, and be with them to develop the plan to create the desired change. For them to say "yes" and want to work with me, they have to believe that I have the capacity to do all these. As a small business owner, I have learned that I need to self-promote in order to build my credibility. I'm not great at self-promotion, so I am learning.

Making a Difference: I could say that I really learned how to leverage the skills that naturally come to me as a woman. When I moved to D.C., I pursued my coaching certification, because I believed, through my own experience with executive coaching, that coaching is a powerful tool that I could use to help others. With coaching, the skills I have gained transformed my life, my relationships, and the quality of relationships I have with people. I took coaching further and developed those skills I think a lot of women naturally possess: being curious, helpful, and being a good listener. All these make for a great consultant. I continue to hone and use them to make a difference.

Mentorship is invaluable. Helping to mentor or coach young and old women, it does not matter what age, results in an openness and willingness to step into their power and claim it. I would encourage women to find someone they can trust—be it a mentor or a coach, someone they can speak their truth and be vulnerable with—and together start to unpack some of the beliefs that are holding them back from being as successful as they can or in being able to influence situations, people, and behaviors. They have to challenge beliefs that come from messages that they got growing up. They have to create new beliefs for themselves.

If we plan to change longstanding patterns in our society around power, then we should shine a light on it and make intentional choices to practice a new form of power—**power that is collective**, so we all have ownership in the results. For instance, we need to challenge the way we look at power—power is not in a limited supply; it is not something that is diminishing.

A great deal of societal elements connected to powerlessness equate to the lack of choices that we have, or we feel we have, in our lives. Anger and frustration stem from lack of choices or perception of the lack of choices.

In this current political climate, women are taking a stand more and more, and it feels safe to do so because there is power in numbers. It is key that we are more intentional and deliberate about the path we take. For one, we need to talk about power—the good, the bad, the ugly, and how it's manipulated. We have to put it in sunshine as we discuss the un-discussable, the unmentionables, those things that make us uncomfortable. If we are ever going to make a change, we have to unpack and understand it all. We then use the information to make conscious choices about how we lead going forward. We are going to be more inclusive. We are going to create a more equitable society, organization, board of directors, or whatever is right in front of us, with the intentional and deliberate choices that we make.

CHAPTER 5

Let's Hear It
from the Men

As was noted before, the strategic goal of this initiative is to offer women guidelines for action to help them navigate the treacherous and largely unchartered journey towards power. To this end, we have designed an essentially female power construct that takes into consideration the innate strengths that women possess, such as solving problems through collaboration and relationship-building, empowering others (sharing power), and searching for win-win outcomes. Our intention is not to focus on the dialectic tension and conflict between women and men, but rather to shine a light on the systematic, intentional, and deliberate ways of acquiring and keeping power for women. There is enough of everything to go around—it would just simply be preferable for men to share the power and influence of a culturally-imposed privilege reserved for a dominant gender. In this section, we will ask men, who have reported positive experiences with women leaders, especially in the workplace and other public spheres of influence, to share their perspective on the new power construct (WomenPower Paradigm) and offer us advice and guidance on how to achieve this elusive goal. It is also an attempt on our part to present a fairly balanced perspective on our proposed female construct of power. George focused on his experience with the one female leader who had the greatest impact and influence on the trajectory and success of his career. Ed, James, Robert and RJ provided us with a panoramic overview of their careers and experiences with women leaders.

A majority of the men we interviewed are from the East Coast and Southeastern regions of the United States, are between the ages of 50 and 65, and are employed/were employed in law enforcement, health care, non-profits, and human resources. We deliberately selected respondents from male-dominated (law enforcement) and female-dominated (health care and nonprofits) occupations to compare and contrast differences in perceptions and observations.

Here's What Men Are Saying: Assessment of the New Womenpower Paradigm

George: On Jessica, the People Person

Jessica would be the fourth unforgettable woman boss I had. But she was my only *mentor.* Throughout my career, I have worked with an equal number of male and female supervisors, advisors, and board presidents. Each could not have been more different from the other; here are three women bosses worth mentioning to highlight how Jessica's leadership stood out.

Armed with a science degree after graduation, I took an offer, almost as a challenge, to work as a writer for the number one public relations agency in Manila. I performed odd jobs for the owner, dubbed as the Queen of PR in the Philippines entertainment scene back in those days. Comfortable meeting people from all walks of life, I enjoyed interviewing celebrities and orchestrating often difficult collaborations among mass media professionals, writers, actors, photographers, and artists. I was not surprised when the queen "promoted" me as a production assistant, a PA, which also meant "personal assistant" in the industry parlance. She had taken on a movie project as a line producer. Unfortunately, I felt more like a personal assistant to her because of the way she spoke to me. She could not make me see the networking and other golden opportunities that awaited me in that job. Perhaps an older me would have simply ignored the office backtalk that prevented me from seeing the windfall to come after working for her on a successful movie project. But at that moment, I felt the stress of dealing with her overbearing personality and sometimes harsh tone, and it was not worth the wait.

Everyone thought I passed up gold, but I also felt that entertainment was the wrong industry for me then.

Determined to put to use my training in biology, I applied for and got a job as a research assistant for a big public health project led by a professor, who was much feared by her graduate students, at a prestigious national university. As a well-respected health education expert, she was asked to return to the university after retirement to continue leading this commissioned project. However, the almost 50-year gap between our career-lives and her reputation as straight-talking, no-nonsense boss proved too intimidating for the younger me, still trying to find his way, so I decided to quit.

Years later, when I had advanced degrees under my belt, I ended up reporting to another accomplished CEO–executive director, this time at a botanical garden, a dream job and workplace for me. She, a well-known scientist and pioneering-researcher, had just published a highly successful memoir, the latest among other major publications. At that time, she was just promoted to the top position after heading a team of other well-known scientists in the garden's esteemed research department. But she attracted controversy as much as she garnered accolades and awards for her work. The general consensus was that whatever power she wielded and amassed, she did for her own gain. She later moved on to several other positions, out of state, shortly after I sought other opportunities for what I hoped would be better working conditions. In my naïve mind then, I craved greater appreciation and support for what I thought I did for the organization I loved.

I chose to write about Jessica, her leadership style, skills, and competencies, because I believe that she brought out the best in me not only as her follower and student, but also as co-worker and teammate. She successfully embodied a leader who inspired good work, even excellence, but not out of fear of reprisal, reprimand, or being shamed by covert put-downs as I had previously experienced working for the other big personalities. I personally did not harbor any resentment reporting to high-powered, assertive women whom others may have perceived as overly ambitious, self-promoting, or in great need of proving something. I know, however, that other co-workers around me did, even though only women discussed the negative more openly.

Jessica never once played the "woman as a victim" card. Instead I believe she took advantage of a slightly motherly tone and appearance that assured me, and most everybody, that we were not in competition, and I was not being perceived as a threat to her.

What skills did Jessica have that commanded respect as a leader? Jessica's listening skills endeared her to co-workers and friends alike. Associates joked that she talked too much, and with great speed too. Often our shoptalk drifted to her one-minute monologues about personal histories that were difficult to mentally track or remember because they happened years before we met and in places unknown to me. But she used those highly condensed narratives to make a point about what she heard me say. They never felt like gossip, because she got to the lessons learned part sooner or later.

She trained as an accountant, because women were not encouraged to major in mathematics, a subject she loved when she was in college. Because she ran the city's history museum (with roughly a $2-million annual budget) as the executive director, and I managed the education programs, we brought up news to each other, including breakthroughs in science. When I did, she listened. She may not have completely understood the content of what I said or what got me excited about it, but she made me feel that she knew how important the news was to me. It was difficult to attribute that solely to her intelligence.

I met Jessica years before she became my boss on a day trip we took together to a beautiful garden in Central Florida where I worked. The friends of the botanical garden group organized this bus tour as a fundraiser. At that time, she was the CEO of a non-profit organization providing care to those with developmental disabilities. She immediately recognized me before I remembered that we had met previously at another reception, when I was an intern, before getting hired by this botanical garden. She instantly addressed me by my title (for having a Ph.D.) and my first name. I thought it was a nice gesture but also felt that Doctor was unnecessary. However, it sure felt good, especially to be remembered. Little did I realize that she had brain memory storage and access capacities that matched a computer! And more importantly, it was how she made me feel that day that actually stayed with me. She recalled whatever information I had told her about me when we first met at that cocktail party!

Her people skills could only be rivaled by her consistency. Other non-profit volunteers and donors would remark that she attended every single fundraising and networking event in the city. She always carried with her a single-use instant camera and took pictures with everybody, long before the selfie-phenomenon. Not one of us ever saw a single picture in print afterwards. We inferred that she had a reference photo-file with our names and profiles.

I believe Jessica excelled in dealing with people. For instance, she knew that someone like me who was just re-starting a career after graduate school did not a donor make. We certainly were also not in the same league professionally, despite my recent academic achievement. Yet she treated me as an equal, with respect and dignity. Later, as we worked together at the history museum, events would put her people and listening skills to the test.

I had been told by the local LGBT community of a cache of photographs documenting years of the history of *Pride* in the area. As the museum's education curator, I decided to display the photographs. Around that time the nearby county's council members voted to take down ALL references to *Pride Parades* from library display windows and announcement boards. My decision to exhibit the photographs on the wall I designated for use by communities became the museum board's heated topic of debate.

To show respect for me as a person and the work of the LGBT community I supported, Jessica allowed me to express my indignation over the controversy in private and fought with the board to keep the exhibit panels. She eventually took down two pictures that were deemed inappropriate. Looking back, it would have been easy for me to walk out. Considering that we, the staff, wrote grants to help us seek underserved audiences and reach out to disadvantaged and marginalized groups, I thought then that photographs of past *Pride Parades* sparking controversy made no sense. But while Jessica validated the many personal emotions attached to several issues that surfaced, she found a compromise, taking the path of least resistance, regardless of her personal opinion. She also did not make a mountain out of the incident. She knew that the *Pride Parade* controversy, like the exhibit, was a temporary preoccupation. "This too will pass," she would say, and laugh.

What Jessica Had to Do: Aside from setting-up exhibits on local history and developing educational activities for special learners, the other fun assignment for me from Jessica involved writing grant applications to support programs and raise capital funds for the museum.

There is an area where Jessica truly excelled. She was a lifelong learner and open to new ways of doing things. More specifically, she kept her mind open to new ideas and encouraged exploration of unanswered questions, new activities, and additional sources of income or donations. She welcomed any demonstration of initiative from the staff and would actually heap words of praise every opportunity she had when ideas, plans, and new assignments went well. She quickly let go of any scheme that failed to take off. But she always made sure that proposed ways of doing business aligned with best practices both in accounting and financial reporting for nonprofits. But all leaders of any enterprise should possess these traits, right? What set Jessica apart was her confidence. She authentically knew what she was doing, so she did not have to pretend in order to convince anyone. As such, she had no qualms about sharing credit and awarding it to any deserving individual.

Although she talked non-stop about herself, her life and relatives, the stories did not resonate as narcissistic or self-promotion. Instead, story-telling times were fun bonding moments, because from deep within she emanated genuine concern for others and the organization's well-being. Always positive and cheerful in tone, she laughed out loud at her misadventures and at her own jokes. She created a congenial, collaborative, and non-judgmental atmosphere. As such, fewer egos clashed in the process.

More importantly, she showed up to work ready and happy. By the time she arrived in the morning, she had already made phone calls to the staff while *en route* to work. When I took over her position because the botanical garden recruited her as an interim CEO–executive director, she kept our line of communication open. She encouraged me to call whenever I had questions. When I did, she would often put me on a brief hold and seconds later return with the answer. She carried a file folder of the museum's vital information and copies of documents with her to the new post, another nonprofit. She advised me to create a similar file folder.

What Could Be Improved? Jessica talked a lot. The amount of words, ideas, and stories she crammed during conversations reflected her life. She had a frenetic energy about her, as if something was about to explode anytime. She ended up "putting out fires," as she would put it, as she solved one problem after another because her sense of urgency applied equally to all tasks. She did not take a breath to allocate time for rest or for bigger planning breaks. Although she carved out time for her weekly beauty rituals, family, and vacation time, she seemed always in a rush. Unfortunately, this may have contributed to some bad eating habits and health problems.

What would I say to women in general? Jessica skillfully deployed a woman's natural nurturing power to win people over and navigate challenging situations. She never played the gender or age card, because not once did she pretend to be a victim. She celebrated her skills, training, and talents to earn for her family and to benefit those dependent on the services provided by the nonprofits she led.

In my experience working with leaders who are men—directors, officers, and board presidents—less talk equated to less emotions. This got the work done faster. Also, talking too much for men can be a double-edged sword. Men can get in trouble very quickly for speaking their minds, unfiltered and without review. Men appear less mindful or considerate of others simply because men were brought up to be less in touch with their emotions. In general, men were told to suppress any outward expressions of what could be perceived as weak. However, I have also observed that leaders showing empathy to others can have lasting positive impacts. Although it comes easier to most women, both men and women can use simple words like, "I hear you" (I care enough to listen to you), which can sound nurturing without requiring too many details.

Men talk less because they are expected to think big. In conversations, men appear to barely hear details, because they await the punch line, eager to react to any life or death implications that will make the information matter to them. Women tend to dwell on details. In my experience, men tended to present big ideas, then they would let me work out the nitty-gritty of methodologies, almost like handing down a command or challenge without instructions. Women on the other hand, remain present and stay actively involved in any conversation about steps to take and choices to make, as if all of the details matter.

While women-talk takes more time, in my opinion, the absence of men in the subsequent discussion of details erodes trust. It is harder to think that leaders (bosses) who are men will keep my best interest in mind as a subordinate male. It is easier to think "to each his own," because people in leadership roles can easily advance their positions before anybody else's. This atmosphere of competition among men may come from the traditional expectation that men are breadwinners for their families. This competitive streak, the "do or die" attitude, "how do I win the next promotion," seems to be more acute in men, and it's not even referred to as ambition. Women on the rise to the top can easily be labeled as ambitious, which is also one reason why women can be more cautious and deliberate. The other extreme is for women to overcompensate. I have seen women leaders make bold statements through actions and the tone in their language. This, to me, made Jessica more admirable. She found the sweet spot, neither operating from a position of timidity nor arrogance. Instead, she highlighted what women do best—dispensing the right amount of nurturing to win people over.

Pam is another leader who worked with Jessica at the botanical garden, and like myself, admires Jessica's style of managing and leading. Her concept of power is summarized in this insightful and profound remark: "If you find a woman who is respected, who is heard, and who listens, you'll find someone very successful. Women like her don't even know they have power. Power is not in their vocabulary because that is not the goal. They don't think about it. They know they have something to do—that which they love to do—and they want to share it and bring other people along. These women have a mission to complete, and they want everybody to be on a team to work equally on that mission. Because they work *with* people, they do not work *for* people, and nobody works *for* them. *With* is a wonderful four-letter word in power and management."

Pam, who worked with two women out of ten supervisors, identifies a woman in a position of power in the workplace as someone capable of making co-workers feel part of a group that has a goal that they want to accomplish together. A leader, according to Pam, is powerful if she can motivate people she works with to do what needs to be done by them.

Knowledge Is Power: "Women are from Venus, men are from Mars," said Pam. She acknowledged that men and women have two very different management styles. Men are single focused, and that is very efficient in business, something women can learn from. But women, aside from being aware of everything, can think with both sides of their brain at the same time. Pam backed up this claim with a story.

"'You build a parking garage for women,' said the man who built the parking garage at the posh St. Armand's Circle in Sarasota," reported Pam. Women sense what is going on around them; it's like having a 360-degree instinctive radar inside them. Lighting, according to the architect, has to be designed for women who look around everywhere all the time. "Women want to know what is coming at them and what is present," observed Pam.

It comes as no surprise then that Pam credited Jessica's success as a leader with her ability to read everyone like a book. "Jessica's magic wand," said Pam, "was that she never forgot what everyone ever said or did." Jessica would find out as much as she could about a person. This included how a person hears information or instructions. She understood that she could not teach anybody unless she knew how he or she learned. She talked to co-workers the way they hear, which means she changed both the verbal and body language she used.

Pam claimed that "knowledge is power." For anyone in a position of power, the best thing to do is get other people to talk about themselves. Jessica knew what others know, their aspirations, or where they want to go. By being herself, she created a situation that made everyone comfortable enough to feel free to talk about themselves or about anything else. According to Pam, no one thought twice about spilling his or her guts to Jessica, and at times, she would come home thinking, "Jessica knows everything about me now!" But Pam believes that this was really good. Pam quickly added that she also felt Jessica's love, as Jessica was a very loving and giving person. "Jessica was always thinking about other people," Pam explained.

Jessica Listened: Jessica's ability to listen appeared intuitive. It almost felt as if this power to listen came through the back door and nobody noticed that she was doing it. "She was so genuinely interested in you or what you were about, that her power came from the knowledge she gained by using her listening techniques," Pam said. But it also came naturally to her. Not very many people have this ability to make listening appear so easy.

"The more you know about other people, the more you know about yourself," Pam emphasized. Jessica made it about the person she was talking with or interviewing, and not about herself. She learned about that person before she did anything else. As such, she knew the job to pick for everyone because she also knew his or her capabilities. She matched the level of education, skills, and learning styles with the assignments she gave. And that was because she had already spent time listening and learning how everyone hears.

Pam knew this from experience. Pam started working with her at a botanical garden before Jessica left to head other nonprofit organizations, and later returned as the garden's CEO–executive director. Jessica worked out very well for Pam as a boss, because she and Jessica had a lot in common. Both had been teachers and were from the South.

After earning a degree in music education, Pam's first job teaching elementary music took her to two all-black schools in Durham, North Carolina. Then she taught music and worked with reading lab students at a community college. In Sarasota, Florida, Pam's jobs prior to the garden were at the Chamber of Commerce, Better Business Council, and the city's biggest hospital. Her work involved writing a newsletter and organizing events for large groups of people. Pam explained that dealing with a hundred different concerns at the same time during large gatherings required listening and multi-tasking skills. Successful teachers study how students learn and hear information. Also, teachers themselves have to learn just about anything in order to teach and pass on the same knowledge or skills.

Pam emphasized that reading people or interpreting behavior, like Jessica did, was never about judging people. Judgment, according to Pam was "when you make a decision about what a person may be, without having enough information."

Jessica Never Left Anyone Behind: Jessica understood human behavior. She was so attuned to human behavior that it did not take her long to get any information that she needed. Moreover, she never left anybody behind. She took everybody that she ever met with her, so you always felt safe with Jessica, because she was always with you. Her whole life, she kept up with what was going on with you all the time. "She was present every day that she could be, as if you were the only person in the world," said Pam of her boss.

"Her personality was so joyous, and as a spiritual person, she wanted the good stuff for everybody. She wanted everybody to succeed. It was not about power to her, rather she believed that one succeeded through other's success. To Jessica, it was always about the welfare of the other person," Pam added. "It reminds me of Maya Angelou's quote about people remembering how you made them feel."

According to Pam, Jessica's leadership skills are intimately related to her gender, chiefly that nurturing comes naturally to women. Pam said, "although men have the same nurturing tendency, it cannot possibly be anywhere near where women have it since men are not capable of doing what women can do—conceive and give birth to a baby—there's a difference," she said.

Pam's career working for nonprofits made her conclude that nonprofit professionals, both men and women, tend to be more nurturing than perhaps those who are in corporate-like settings. The healing mission of all nonprofits may have to do with this. In nonprofits or in academia, the process is just as important as the product or end result. Whereas, in the corporate world, Pam remarked, "it does not matter how you get to the end—the process does not matter as much—just get there and get the goods. Only the bottom line counts. I think a lot of men are happier in that kind of situation because they don't have to be emotionally attached. It is easier for women to be attached."

What Should Change? According to Pam, "everybody has a management style. Jessica's style all plays together with her being a woman. Men have management styles different from hers, because men value other things in the business place. Men have to eliminate a handful of steps or processes, because they have to get to the bottom line quicker and deadlines are less flexible. It's more of a sink or swim scenario in the corporate world."

Pam's Advice to Women: Pam advises us to "find a teacher or someone who can be that powerful person we model ourselves after. Whether these teachers ever stepped in a classroom or not, they are our guides. Find someone who you want to be like, someone who does what you love to do well, that someone you admire, whom you feel safe and comfortable to talk with. Have two or three role models who can show and tell you what to do, then pattern yourself after them."

"If you fill your life with the positive, then there isn't any room for the negative. Stick to the people whom you admire. You don't want to be guided by people only out for themselves, because you want to feel like part of a team or a community," Pam concluded.

James and Ed's Assessment of the Womenpower Paradigm

James and Ed are currently working for a nonprofit agency serving individuals with disabilities in the capital city of Dover, Delaware. I interviewed them, because I am familiar with their rich and diverse work history, their leadership and work styles, and their keen abilities to provide analysis and fresh perspectives on this specific topic. James has worked as a social worker and a top administrator for both nonprofit and governmental agencies in both the states of Pennsylvania and Delaware. When I shared with him the four elements of the **Character** component of the WomenPower Paradigm, he completely agreed that women leaders who are aspiring to gain power must know who they are and do their work to benefit others and to benefit the common good, but he was hesitant about the 4th element—pursuit of the truth, especially objecting to the use of the word "relentless." He said to drop "relentless" because in our lofty pursuit of the truth, we sometimes badger people, antagonize them, and forget about the end goal. He also added that when we acquire power, we need to *share it* and empower others to act. He noted that it is the responsibility of the leader to grow and nurture people.

James agreed with the eight **Competencies** identified in the WomenPower Paradigm. He gave an example of a supervisor who failed to gain power because of low emotional intelligence, underdeveloped people skills, and an inability to balance strength with kindness. Sometimes, he recounted, the executive was ineffective because she was using "pure heart" as a way to manage people, which then led her to tread on the wrong path. He discussed another woman leader, who was his supervisor when he worked as a vocational rehabilitation counselor. She was fairly young but smart, confident, and highly competent. The leader knew herself, was completely self-assured, stood by her principles, and supported her people. James recalled an incident when a client complained about him. The leader asked the client to choose who to partner with. She supported James by framing the question in such a way that the legitimate choice was right in front of the recalcitrant client. She calmly asked the client to choose between "Mr. James, who is the best man for the job, or another one with less experience." The leader invariably supported her employees when she knew they were right. She always made them feel valued, competent, and trusted.

Ed is a highly trained and experienced community and economic development professional with work experience in Pennsylvania, Arizona, and Delaware. He is currently working as the marketing and development specialist for a nonprofit agency in

Dover, Delaware. He was in agreement with the eight **Competencies** listed as major components of the WomenPower Paradigm. He suggested that it might be wise to add community building as a key competency that women need to adopt and harness to gain power. He cited people skills, conflict resolution and political skills as paramount to achieving power and influence. Subject matter expertise in leadership positions in any organization is also a critical requirement, according to Ed. For example, it's problematic to be a top executive if the individual lacks training and experience in management, leadership, and financial management.

When he was in Pennsylvania, Ed worked with four high-powered women, all with solid training in areas needed by the Latino organization that they were working for. The executive director was a lawyer, trained at Georgetown University in Washington, D.C. Another held a doctoral degree from the University of Michigan, and the deputy director was a graduate of Swarthmore College, with expertise in psychology. All three were highly competent, aggressive women, who enjoyed wielding power. They all appeared to have leadership styles of early women leaders, who had to fight to grab power, be highly trained, competent and experienced, and who engaged in a free-for-all struggle with men and women of that historical period. This happened in the early 1990s, when women first moved into leadership positions, with no role models except the hierarchical garden-variety type of male dominance. It was a time when social norms, workplace structure and function, and women's leadership roles were slowly getting redefined. Radical ideas and militancy were needed to usher in a new era for women's leadership in the workplace. At that time, Margaret Thatcher, the "Iron Lady," was the prevailing model of power for women leaders. These three women leaders were simply a product of that era. They were the right leaders for the right time. However, in the 21st century, a new model of power needs to be developed, tested and adopted that takes into consideration the foundational **Character and Competency components** of the WomenPower Paradigm.

Larry Trunfio:
Perspective from an HR Practitioner

According to a longitudinal study conducted by William Scarborough, *What the Data Says About Women in Management Between 1980 and 2010* (Primary Source: U.S. Census and the American Community Survey: 1980–2010), 60 percent of management positions in the human resources field are occupied by women. This figure increased from the low rate of 35 percent in 1980, a phenomenal 71.4 percent increase in a 30-year period. Although there still exists a 10 percent gender wage gap in this field, the predominance of women in HR managerial positions could prove to be a positive factor in promoting gender equity and diversity.

Larry is a training administrator for the Department of Human Resources of the State of Delaware. He is an expert in quality improvement techniques, organizational development, and leadership training. I interviewed him because of his expert knowledge in leadership and management and his extensive experience working with remarkable and highly competent women of power. What a perfect combination! In the HR department where he works, there are five women directors out of seven, and the cabinet secretary, the top executive, is a woman. Larry is accustomed to reporting to women leaders and has had positive experiences interacting with and reporting to them. All his responses appear to be in complete agreement with the **WomenPower** Paradigm that I shared with him. He noted that "self-awareness is critical in developing trust and is fundamental to leadership. Self-knowledge increases confidence in oneself." He pointed out that exercising power to benefit others is vitally important. He added that "when managers and leaders are using power to benefit themselves, then it becomes difficult to create an effective team." He asserted that when managers focus on teamwork and collaboration, it is far more effective in getting employees to follow the leaders to implement their vision, because employees are motivated to act for the team. He concluded that "it's absolutely necessary to pursue the truth, because without it everything becomes debatable and gray. This causes confusion and it does not bring us

111

together. Some leaders," he added, "manipulate other people. In the short-term, it could be effective, because people follow out of fear. However, it's not effective in the long-term."

There was true fidelity between his responses and the competency matrix that I shared with him. He was in complete agreement with the eight selected competencies, tempered with the keen awareness that these competencies might change depending on the dimensions of time, context, external political, economic and social factors, and customer needs and requirements. Intentional adaptive changes could be made by reviewing the framework on an ongoing basis and with predictable frequency, say every two years or so. Larry asserted that management and leadership are big concepts, and to effectively wield power, women "must balance both." He added, "you cannot manage people without being a leader. However, it's also important not to micro-manage employees." According to Larry, "communication is an important competency to have. You cannot do anything by yourself. You need to give and receive information to be able to manage and lead."

Larry feels that women might be better at developing emotional intelligence and connecting with people. He recounted that "based on experience, women are more adept at problem solving. They give people power to solve their own problems and not wait for someone to tell them what to do." In terms of conflict resolution, he remarked that "women are less directive, more open-ended, and collaborative. They focus on relationships rather than tasks. Leaders must address the conflict before the environment gets hostile." He segued into a short excursus on political power as an important skill to possess and that women must identify the power structure, not necessarily positional power. However, he added, "some women choose not to play the game."

Larry noted that "competence and knowledge are more easily granted to men than to women leaders. Women need to be twice as good to get the same respect." He might be on to something that recent research has verified as an emerging pattern. According to a study conducted by the Pew Research Center (Parker, 2018), there are significant differences in gender discrimination

tied to gender makeup in the workplace. For example, 37 percent of women who work in a mostly male workplace reported that
they have been treated as if they were *not competent* by virtue of
their gender. Likewise, the women in the study reported getting
less support from their senior leaders than a man (24 percent versus 12 percent). Larry suggested that one vital path to gaining
power and influence is the use of mentoring programs. "Women
value it more than men," he added. Finally, Larry proclaimed that
women are more effective as a "collective rather than as an individual. A majority of the division directors in the department where
I work are women. Together, they have been able to make significant changes. They are more effective and powerful when they work
together."

Women Leaders in Male-Dominated Occupations

What challenges do women face in male-dominated occupations, such as law enforcement, engineering, architecture and IT?
Are these barriers magnified when women assume leadership positions? A survey of U.S. adults conducted in 2017 by the Pew Research
Center indicated that women employed in majority-male workplaces encountered high rates of gender discrimination when it
comes to fair treatment in recruitment and hiring (48 percent), fair
treatment in promotion and advancement (38 percent), and workplace attention paid to increasing gender diversity (49 percent).
Gender makeup in the workplace is also linked to all forms of discrimination, such as "being treated as if you were not competent"
(37 percent), "earning less than a man" (35 percent), or "receiving less support from senior leaders" (24 percent). Below are interviews with two police officers giving their perceptions and advice on
how women leaders can maximize their chances of success in the
male-dominated law enforcement profession. Let's listen to their
voices.

Robert: On Women Leaders
in Law Enforcement

"When my boss got promoted, the sheriff had the discretion to either give her a 5% or a 10% increase for the promotion. My boss found out that all of her male counterparts had been given 10% and she, only a 5% pay raise," Robert narrated, in a matter-of-fact tone. "I believe she filed an EEOC (Equal Employment Opportunity Commission) complaint all the way to the regional office in Atlanta. That judge ruled against her." Robert added, with the same even tone, "the judge said that the sheriff had the choice to do whatever he wanted."

"It just seems unfair," Robert continued. "Of course, after my boss filed that complaint, it was downhill from there—no more promotion or anything for her. She was vanished from downtown to a street job, albeit in the same position, as a supervisor. The sheriff just wanted her to go away—get out of the building—he didn't want to see her; he didn't want to have anything to do with her!"

Robert, who recently retired as deputy for a traditionally elected sheriff in a Florida county with roughly 1.1 million residents, believes that times have changed. But he contends that politics will remain the same. He had seen it all. He worked for 25 years in law enforcement. He joined when he was 20 and retired at 45, after extending service five more years. "In 1985 when I started, women were already integrated into the force but there weren't many women supervisors—few, not very many of them." Robert remembers that during the early part of his career in the 80s and part of the 90s, captain was the highest rank among the women deputies. It wasn't until later that women were promoted to the rank of major. "I believe that the one who was a major started out at a jail facility," he said.

"Law enforcement was a predominantly male, if not an all-male, profession then. Now, the chief deputy (second to the sheriff) of the county is female, and there is a female colonel as well—both are pretty substantial, or high position and rank. But there has never been a female sheriff (the elected or appointed top position) in the county. We hope soon, but not yet."

Women and Minorities on the Force: "I can't imagine how

difficult it is for a woman to enter a male-dominated workforce," Robert said. Although women entered the field more than 100 years ago, there are only 12.5 percent female law enforcement officers in this profession, according to an FBI Report issued in 2017. Robert compared the status of policewomen with women firefighters. He remarked, "back in the firemen days, station houses were set up for men. The bathroom and sleeping arrangements satisfied the needs of an all-male force. Fire departments nationwide have transitioned and made adjustments to welcome more females." Yet, according to Robert, news as recent as two years ago revealed that female fighters still encounter privacy issues at fire stations.

"Same thing with law enforcement. Just imagine the conversations—locker room talk—topics that men banter about a lot," Robert added. "It was so infrequent to have female colleagues. I think I could count with my hands how many women I interacted with on a given shift of any kind." Moreover, in the late 80s according to Robert, it was also not uncommon for a homeowner to call the office or dispatch back and say, "I want a real deputy," which, Robert said, meant a white deputy. Back then, an African American deputy responding to a home break-in surprised homeowners in some, although not all, parts of the county. Robert quickly added, however, that the sheriff's office would of course say something like, "well ma'am you have a deputy, if you don't want that deputy you don't have a crime to report."

"Women who are gay do much better in those male-dominated positions in law enforcement than gay men. Oh, totally!" Robert mused. "Because the minute they (members of unit) find out that you are a gay male, they won't be overt to your face, but because behind the scenes they have the power to do whatever they want, they usually do," Robert explained. "I had seen what they did to a young man who joined the department, and who was openly gay. He made no qualms about it. He lasted very, very little time. I mean they did everything and anything. They found something wrong with everything he did, and that literally drove him crazy. There was nothing he could do about the situation. I don't think there was a gay male who went beyond my rank. I think I was the highest rank for a gay male, a master sergeant." Asked if he himself was out, Robert said: "No, I did my job and I went home; that was it. My private life was my business. I rarely spent time with work-friends outside of work or anything like that. That was a totally different era. I got promoted on my 17th year as deputy," said Robert.

Ever since he was a little kid, Robert always wanted to be a police officer. Every Christmas he would ask his mother to buy him a police uniform at the local store in town because, first, the costume was on sale—it was left over from Halloween—and second, because he dreamt of being a cop one day. "Officer Friendly," the outreach cop, who brought coloring books and talked to kids, had a major impact on little Robert when he was in primary school. Robert thought Officer Friendly was a nice guy, and this impression sealed his fate.

"My parents came from Cuba in 1958. They met here in the U.S., in New Jersey. We didn't actually speak English until I went to kindergarten," Robert explained. They lived in a predominantly Spanish neighborhood. If not for the cartoons Robert watched at home in English, all interactions with friends, other families, and with everybody else around him were all in Spanish. Because he spoke English before everybody else, he was the translator of the family. "When the phone rang at home, I had to answer. If something came in the mail to read or an issue needed to be resolved, I had to be there. I was there for the closing and sale of the house." The idea of helping out and being a leader were ingrained in him early on.

Robert's family moved to Florida when he was 14. He finished junior high school and high school, and then briefly went to the county's community college. His mother worked as a seamstress, and his father was an auto factory employee. They could not afford to continue to send him to college. "So, I got the job at the Sheriff's office, and luckily, they paid for my education. I got my bachelor's from a private university. I am very appreciative of that—education afforded me a lot of opportunities that I don't think I had seen before," Robert effusively expressed.

"But here I was, I've been with the force for 17 years. I had never been in trouble. I did my job, did everything I was told, took the promotional examinations, and it took me 17 years to get promoted,"

Robert said. "I am Hispanic at that, and bilingual, yet it took me 17 years to get promoted," he emphasized. "It wasn't until a female lieutenant above me advocated for me strongly that I got promoted, or I probably would not have gotten promoted in rank."

So How Does One Climb the Ladder to a Position of Power? "The thing about this type of (paramilitary) job is that chiefs are not normally going to hire someone from the outside to just come in and be the supervisor," Robert said. Bosses, male or female, rose from the ranks and were therefore colleagues that deputies had worked with, side by side. By the time someone got promoted, most everybody would have already known what he or she was capable of doing. "You know their personalities, you know what bothers them, so nothing is unfamiliar," Robert added.

"For any job position in the force, regardless of gender, it is competency that matters. If one shows competency in the job they do, there's really no issue with gender, but if you're not competent, it's going to be a disaster. Even when it came to my female supervisor, I had, by the time of her appointment, known that she was competent and capable. I didn't have an issue with her gender. I can't think of any problems I personally had with a female supervisor treating me like a subordinate, or in which I felt that," Robert said.

Females on the force had also mentioned to him, according to Robert, that they had absolutely no problems working with men. In fact, women supervisors preferred working with men, he said. If a woman were supervising men, say a female sergeant supervisor, there was going to be less resistance because men saw themselves as soldiers. "Men will say, 'yes ma'am,' move on, and be done with whatever she said. Females, not so much," Robert chimed. Sometimes fellow female subordinates questioned the boss's directives.

Do Women Have an Equal Shot? "Everybody in the force, regardless of gender, received the same training. Everyone has the same equipment," Robert said. However, women "don't get any breaks." They still have to do all that men do physically. "I don't know how fair that is because I am 6 ft., 190 lbs.; I don't have a problem dragging a 180 lb. dummy to however many yards. But you have a female deputy, and she is expected to drag the dummy the same distance I did in the same time frame. Women don't get any slack." Robert explained that part of expectations about women being equal in physical strength to those of men is that a deputy can lose his or her life out in the streets. If a partner cannot drag an injured colleague who got shot, then he or she is unable to help. If any female wanted to do law enforcement work, then she did as everyone else. "There are no short cuts," Robert said.

One of the most important skills required in law enforcement, according to Robert, is the ability to communicate well and talk to people. That could help defuse a tense situation. "Most people just want to be heard," he emphasized. "Women can have a way with people. Chances are a 6 ft., 300 lb. guy, angry at the world, is not going to beat up on the female cop that comes over. Again, this has to do with how you talk to people," Robert repeated. "A little compassion goes a long way, even with the bad guy."

He further extolled the good qualities of women applicable to successful law enforcement and leadership. As a field training officer, Robert had a female co-trainer, and also had a female in the car while training cadets. From this experience, he observed that women "get it" or understand concepts more intuitively. "I found that more males didn't have common sense; and one of the things you can't teach is common sense; you either have it or you don't," he said. "Females are very good at multi-tasking and they are very good at managing their time. Males for whatever reason could not multi-task and couldn't get things accomplished on time," Robert claimed. Because a typical workday could be responding to call after call after call, some men are just unable to handle all else that goes with the workload. "Some could not remember what reports needed to be written just as another call came in, whereas females are generally more meticulous about taking notes and remembering things to do while on other tasks," Robert emphasized.

"It's amazing to me that men would complain more than women do," Robert observed. "Typically, women officers, who may have two kids at home, shoulder the same responsibilities that go with family life and a full-time law enforcement job that requires them to be away from home for periods of time. Moreover, men and women in law enforcement have reason to get burnout."

A woman's ability to juggle different tasks and to successfully manage sudden increases of workload without complaining much, plus her intuitive people and interpersonal communication skills, prepare her well for law enforcement work. In a system that demands the same level of knowledge, competencies, and physical abilities from all candidates, regardless of gender or marital status, women candidates appear to have a chance at leadership. However, societal or cultural expectations require women to perform traditional roles at home or in the domestic realm, which means that they have to work even harder for these leadership positions. Several factors work in favor of women aspirants. In a competitive promotion system within a hierarchical structure, competition among women for certain positions is nil or non-existent because women on the force are far fewer in number. Women could get the position they apply for when competing with other women.

Robert also mentioned that during down times at work, a lot of men on the force confide in their female co-workers, seeking to know their perspective on matters like relationships. Although the observation may not be supported by evidence, according to Robert, "for sure there's fraternizing back and forth between genders." Many couples met and married while both working in law enforcement, he added. This not only promotes trust and mutual sharing of knowledge; it also shows how much female wisdom is valued even in a male-dominated scene. More importantly, women can gain additional insights on human behavior in the process.

The Road to Promotion: "You have to signify your interest to be promoted or someone has signified interest in getting you promoted," Robert said that is the first step on the path to any position of power for both men and women on the force. "You need to put in a certain amount of time in a grade (level) and then take written tests for promotion. Now, testing has gotten a little more intricate. If you want to be promoted, bosses assign you tasks, say, 'write a memo' to see if you have writing skills. You answer questions from board panelists who give you scenarios, for them to see how you would respond or handle a situation. A lot of the training we do as deputies involve 'what if' scenario-envisioning exercises—those help with advance planning, mental preparation, and problem solving," Robert explained.

"You have to go through all the tests, *but* you need to have an inside track to the promotion. A lot of times it is political. It's about who you know," Robert emphasized. What notoriously happens at times, according to him, is that a deputy could be getting along well with his or her immediate supervisor, but may not be on good terms with the supervisor's superior, who is also the deputy's boss. So, that superior can use the immediate supervisor to either make a notation in an evaluation or do something negative to compromise the deputy's promotion. "Everything is political; again, it depends on who you know." And Robert, speaking rhetorically, added: "Did you go fishing with him? Did you go hunting with him?"

Women Promoted to Positions of Power: "You could tell who the popular supervisors were and the unpopular ones," said Robert. The sign-up board of in-demand supervisors would fill up fast when deputies bid for a squad assignment. According to him, success as a leader has a lot to do with how these supervisors treat others. "Deputies and police officers may look tough and arrogant on the outside, but inside they are like big babies, like kids—every single one of them," Robert revealed. "So, a good leader must treat everybody the same. You can't have preferential treatment or the 'kids' will throw a tantrum."

When Robert himself got promoted after 17 years on the force, he knew exactly who to model himself after, and the kind of boss not to be. One attribute of a good leader for Robert was having a short memory, an ability to disconnect and to quickly move on. While it was important to be timely in providing feedback, a good sense of timing also goes a long way. A good leader to Robert was someone "who did not make it seem like it's the end of the world when one messed up." A leader may be spontaneous and may use harsh language, or even curse when reprimanding subordinates, but a good leader will not harp on it a year later and thereafter. Looking back, Robert elaborated, "one of the best lessons I learned from a supervisor I admired came in the form of advice." From the get go, this supervisor told Robert that "if you are gonna work for me, better have a thick skin and a short-term memory."

"This may work a lot easier for men, I don't know," Robert said. But a good leader, according to him, should have the ability to disconnect. "I was a soldier. I didn't have any problems taking orders or anything like that. I went to work, did my job, and went home. I knew which side of my bread was buttered, and because I didn't want to go anywhere else, my plan was to do my time, get out, and enjoy the rest of my life after retirement."

A Leader Knows Her or His Team: "My best management advice for any CEO is if you wouldn't put somebody at the front counter of your business to provide customer service, then you probably should not have them as your leader. You can put them where they interact with less people," Robert added. "If you're talking about leadership then it is about the ability to motivate people." A good leader knows his or her squad well enough to do that.

"Too many times people are just burned out, especially in law enforcement. Most have been in the service and in the same position for a long time. They have seen everything. Someone may have died that day, but it's the same 'death.' Only the name has changed," Robert spoke from experience. He, like others, had seen the grief, the horror, and all the sadness for decades.

Just like medical doctors, officers need to be detached. "They say that some deputies have good bedside manners and some don't, but that's because people have different ways of coping with life or death situations," Robert said. Knowledge of where every member of the squad is, physically and emotionally, is key. This knowledge leads to a certain degree of flexibility in decision-making, giving assignments, and implementing rules. Flexibility is another important attribute of a successful leader.

"I had a deputy working for me who was totally burned out. My phone kept ringing with calls coming from everywhere he went. People he dealt with complained to me that he was rude, or he was this or that," Robert narrated. "So, I pulled him out and said, 'Why don't we do this: we have a problem with panhandling. Why don't you go and start interviewing these people—talk to them, find out why they are panhandling, and then let's get the resources to help them.'"

"This was the time when all kinds of panhandlers were standing at every single corner begging for money. They were all over the place, and the county was looking to pass an ordinance to get them off the streets. But the real problem is that most of the panhandlers won't get help because the resources were centralized downtown. Most of the homeless have carts with all of their belongings, so they wouldn't go anywhere near downtown."

"So, we opted to bring all the resources to them, or closer to them, as opposed to the other way around. If there were some who badly needed help, I just had the deputy (now energized) to go put the homeless in the car, take him or her downtown, and stand in line with them for four hours (however long it took) until they were able to go and talk to somebody about getting some food stamps or whatever it was they needed. Our assistance evolved; we are now taking them to get state IDs, to the Veterans Affairs (VA), or to the Social Security Office. To this day, the Sheriff's Office has a program called *Homeless Initiative.*" Because of the deputy's efforts, there was a lot less panhandling and the initiative caught on and minimized the incidence of this chronic problem.

What Motivates Law Enforcers? Real-life law enforcers are far more caring than the characters depicted on TV. Robert continued to talk about changes that the *Homeless Initiative* brought. "Deputies go out of their way now to find help—like housing, drug counseling, and health care for the homeless," Robert explained. "Our number one problem with mental health cases here is that the people we take in for evaluation are quickly released as soon as the crisis or breakdown is over. By law, we have to release them. Even when they are told to come back for a follow-up doctor's visit, they seldom ever do. Medications can take three to four weeks to fully kick-in. So, we try to track them down and work with them individually to make sure they show up for their subsequent appointments. It's almost like full time guardianship of these individuals. We have to do it, otherwise they are never gonna get any better."

Is the motivation about helping other people? "Yes! And it's about making a difference," Robert responded. "I always thought the role of an officer is more of a guardian as opposed to an enforcer. It's not uncommon for a deputy to take money out of his own pocket to pay for the fees to acquire a state ID (around $25 plus tax), someone's electric bill, or to buy some groceries for a family. It's not that folks who run out of gas aren't paying attention. It's because they don't have money. A deputy, with whom I went to the academy and whom I ended up supervising, talked about how many times he filled somebody's gas tank without ever mentioning it to anyone. There are a lot of good officers who are out doing some really good things for people, which go unnoticed and will never get recognized." In reality, Robert, like most deputies, are in law enforcement work because they want *to help others.*

What a Leader Should Not Be: Robert was clear on what a good leader is not. He consciously modeled himself after supervisors who treated him fairly and made him feel good about work. He also identified what he did not want to be when he became one. "Cops are like rubberneckers—like those who would slow down on the highway just to have a closer look at an accident. When cops hear that there is a shooting somewhere and they are not doing anything in particular, even though they may not be assigned to the shooting, and they are not supposed to be there, cops always think, 'I'm still *gonna* go, I *wanna* go, I *wanna* see.' Everyone wants to gawk, we're gawkers."

It is not entirely a bad thing. "Sometimes unexpected things happen at the scene in those situations—like a crowd forming and officers there immediately need help with crowd-control," Robert said. "But we had one particular supervisor.... She was just the most gruff and curt of all. Even in those situations she would yell, 'What the fuck are you all doing here?!'" Robert felt that she was trying to show off and demonstrate that she was as tough as all the guys. "But it really backfired," Robert continued. "There were very few people who understood or liked her. She just turned people off with that attitude."

Robert revealed, "In law enforcement, a larger percentage of women are lesbians. They are already prone to having that alpha personality, so to speak." He also noted, "Women get a bad rap. If women were strong-willed or had an opinion, people would say that she's a bitch, but if a guy were the same way, then it's 'Oh, he's great!'"

Advice to Women Aspiring to Claim Positions of Power: "I think it is very good for an organization to send their newly promoted leaders to a leadership school," Robert suggested. The path to promotion in rank may be clearly laid out. But according to Robert, the dynamics totally changed upon assuming any position of power. Many times, candidates who pass the requirements and know how to do their jobs are thrown into leadership positions without any training in leadership skills. To Robert, it could feel like, "Hey you're in-charge now, and you don't have a clue as to what that means, so you're on your own!" A leadership academy or program, for men and women, can teach law enforcers how to become effective and successful leaders all the way to the top.

To the aspiring leader, however, Robert suggested finding a *mentor*. "Number one is to find a mentor who can teach you to communicate and deal with people successfully," he emphasized. "I always tell everyone to be prepared." Even for those considering a career in law enforcement or government service, it is important to network and volunteer. To those aspiring to leadership roles, it is even more important to get involved in the community. "Elected officials run for office, and they will eventually run again. So, it is important to ask yourself if you've already met them, or if you would even consider volunteering for their campaign. These officials may not know you now, but if you show up at a couple of events, they will," Robert said. Being prepared is all about networking after all other requirements have been met. With more women entering careers in law enforcement, with tenacity, hard work, and single-minded focus, it's possible for any woman to gain the competence and solid experience to hold a sheriff's position in the near future.

Officer RJ's Advice to Women: "You Can Do It!"

Retired New York Police Department (NYPD) Officer RJ's advice to women on the way to the top: "Don't take no for an answer! Keep going with total persistence. Set your goal. Get there. You will learn all the ins and outs along the way."

"I don't understand this whole gender bias thing," Officer RJ said with a strong, confident, yet cheerful tone. "There is zero reason why a woman can't do the same exact job as a man. How can I say that women are exactly equal to men? The mentality is the same—it's the same thoughts, the same ideas, and the same goals! I never ever saw a female boss as 'just' a female boss. She was a boss, first and last. To me a boss is a boss in a boss situation. Afterwards, if we went out for beers and hung out, like all the other guys do, then she's female again."

Officer RJ held this very perspective when he became a squad leader, a position of power and responsibility. "I had to treat everybody under me, male and female, the same," he said. "This is why I say to any woman who wants to go after anything, anything at all, 'Set your goals and get it, you can do it. Don't believe in 'the ceiling' falsehood. If you've got to knock down a thousand walls, knock down a thousand and one, because men are expected to do the same." According to a nationwide study led by the Pew Research Center, in collaboration with the National Police Research Platform, however, 43 percent of female officers responded that when it comes to assignments and promotions, men are treated better than women.

"Don't get me wrong. Definitely within the police department, I know that there have been women harassed numerous times—all kinds of harassment from sexual to everything in-between. Women have a hard time. And I understand that. I truly understand the situation," RJ countered. "Women, especially those in leadership positions, have to work just a little bit harder." In a male dominated field, women sometimes need to show more aggression, according to RJ, if only to let peers know that they are on equal footing with other leaders who are men. But successful women leaders are never as aggressive with subordinates. RJ acknowledged the real and perceived challenges faced by women in the force.

While many women in the police department may have struggled, RJ said that many, many more have shined. "Oh yes, there were many successful women in the New York City Police Department." NYPD, considered a paramilitary organization, or almost military in structure and culture, is the 9th largest army in the world, according to RJ. At the time of his service, NYPD had almost over 40,000 members of all different ranks. "There is room for women leaders to shine," RJ emphasized.

No Pay Difference: In a military-like set-up with a specified chain of command, it is crucial for all to respect the rank. As such, most would honor the rank first, then the person. "The boss being a woman would not matter if most realized that rank as well as the person are to be respected," RJ continued. "I don't see 100% alignment to that yet, but I would say that 60% of the department follow this line of thinking. Personally, I'm a little biased; I think the NYC police department is the best in the world." RJ also claimed that no difference in pay rate between men and women existed. "Not in New York City, at least not within the system of promotion. The system is designed so everybody at a particular rank gets paid a certain amount. The structure keeps the pay equal. But, outside this system, I would definitely agree that there could be some inequality."

Again, gender does not matter, according to RJ, at the patrolling level of work in particular. "You are involved, especially on a one-on-one basis, with a patrol partner. With the eight hours you spend together in a radio car, you get to know your partner well. You also see if there's no mesh between you two, or if it's a bad fit," RJ said. "I had many great partners working in the police department—awesome people, and not all of them were males. In fact, I had a few female partners, who I had as much respect for as any male officers, because I've seen them do everything that they needed to do to do their job right. I never worried about my safety, because they had my back, and I had theirs. Gender makes no difference, if the skill level is where it should be."

"There's a place for women to shine, definitely," RJ said. Based on the system, promotion to the captain level rank is determined by performance on tests. "If a female officer were to master the examinations to get to the rank that she needed to get to (the level of captain) and shine from that point forward, then the sky is the limit. Women can be deputy inspectors, inspectors, deputy chiefs, and chiefs—all the way up to the four-stars chief rank, which is the highest-ranking chief before she could become a commissioner. I knew several females who were chiefs. In fact, I knew two black female chiefs, which is even more interesting, because a lot of times minorities don't get to these levels. So yes, they struggled, and they paid their dues. They showed up, and they were phenomenal," RJ proclaimed.

RJ's Journey: "If you really think about it, we police officers do not get to hear that we helped people. A lot of times it's, 'Oh, firemen save lives,' that we hear. They get all the respect. Law enforcement gets a bad rap because we 'arrest people,' and 'we take freedoms away.' Yes, that is one part of the job, but there are many others," RJ revealed. It is the "many others"—like helping those in need the most, which RJ said kept him on the job beyond the five years he intended to stay. RJ, now retired for 11 years, started working for NYPD in 1987. "I went into law enforcement, because my parents were big on taking city exams. Getting a city job so you could get a pension later in life was huge to us then. Law enforcement is an extremely stable one," he said. "I'll do this for five years, and I'll get out. That was my thought then. But once I got involved, five years turned to seven, and seven years turned to ten, because I was having fun."

Officer RJ called meeting and dealing with people "fun." But he also loved the camaraderie. "When you join the Police Department, you join one big family, so it's like you have your regular family at home, then you have your work family," he said. "I also believe that the law has to be enforced—without law there is anarchy. I was big into that belief. My parents brought us up with rules and regulations, and that upbringing transcended into a law enforcement career."

Helping others in situations where "most people don't get help" is to RJ the main reason he stayed. "I was called to a supermarket once, and they (staff) were holding this young girl who had two little kids with her for theft. She stole meat and food. The supermarket staff wanted us to arrest her. When I met her, I was like, 'What's going on?' She just went into tears. She said, 'My kids have nothing to eat, I have no way of getting help. I don't know what to do.' So, my partner and I convinced the supermarket not to press charges. We actually paid for some food for her, not a whole lot. Then, we actually gave her some information on how to get food stamps and do things like that. Sure enough, she came back to us a couple of months later to thank us and tell us that she was in a work program, that she was getting help and that everything was working for her."

RJ recalled that he had many experiences like that on the job. And so did his colleagues, who he said would not think twice about risking their own lives to save others. "I know personally some guys who dove into freezing, ice-cold water before the fire department or anyone else got to the scene to save a kid in a half-frozen lake. And these guys have kids of their own at home!" Saving a drowning child's life or talking to a despondent adult about to jump off a building are some of what police officers do daily, RJ added.

Women Leading Men and Women Dedicated to Helping Others: What does it take to lead? To RJ, successful leaders are those who are in complete control, but are compassionate at the same time. He or she knows how to balance being authoritative and humane. "A leader's power lies in being able to understand people, like what is going on with your subordinates," RJ said. Anyone in a leadership role has only as much power as the respect he or she receives from followers. It is, according to RJ, about understanding the point of view of those led, while being completely knowledgeable of the law and what leaders are expected to do according to those rules and regulations.

In law enforcement, a paramilitary organization, officers are expected to respect the rank and follow the chain of command regardless of the person in the position. But leaders who shine are those respected not only for rank, but also for who they are as a person. Leaders are respected for the quality of their leadership, according to RJ. Since the relationship between superior and subordinate is predetermined by the hierarchical structure, followers are more inclined to respect the process by which this leadership position was attained, that is, through years of experience. "Quality leadership" means leadership seasoned with experience. "Going up through the ranks, leaders learn from the mistakes they've made along the way, and this makes them extremely good at what they do," RJ said.

RJ worked directly under one of the two African American women chiefs in the NYPD. He beamed as he described her: "She knew everything that she needed to know. She was on the ball! It was amazing how much she knew, the knowledge was there," RJ mused. Leaders are respected for the quality of their leadership based on their knowledge competencies. But RJ also noted that, "these women were very powerful and well respected, because they were compassionate toward their employees—male and female."

RJ recalled, "there was one lieutenant I had. She had been on the job many years before I was hired. I believe she had 15 to 20 years ahead of me. Back then, not many women had that rank (lieutenant), so she was really tough; she actually scared a lot of cops. She had to be 'one of the boys.' She actually smoked a little cigar, walked around as a 'tough girl.' Yet still, she got the job done. And that's how people respected her. She held the respect of all the police officers under her rank, because they understood that she was the boss, and you did what she told you to do. That was the old school type of leadership then. But I've also dealt with other female bosses—chiefs, deputy chiefs, or those high-ranking inspectors—who were actually of the more modern type. They were the more intellectual leaders. But they still held respect from subordinates because they were kind, without being overbearing like the mother-type. They behaved like bosses even though they appeared more understanding. They talked through the problems with us more so than what the old type lieutenant would do." RJ said that the veteran lieutenant would have simply told us to "just do this!"

Quality leadership to RJ meant that leaders "knew what subordinates were going through, so they actually knew what to assign to whom that day. Quality leaders listened and really took to heart what people said. And I'm not only talking about female bosses," RJ said. Good leaders did not become "so part of the hierarchy" that they saw "us" and "them." They possessed information, knowledge, and wisdom, which they balanced with compassion.

"You don't have to be so rigid as a leader. When you understand your role, you find out where your subordinates are going, or what's going on with them. So, you become flexible. Especially at patrolling levels, a boss would see if, say, someone who had a bad day came in and was really not up to snuff. Or if a subordinate said, 'I can't handle

129

today's work.' A good boss would say, 'OK, you work inside the building today instead of being out there on the street.'"

RJ recalled, "a family member was actually dying, and I went to the boss, a female boss, to say, 'Look, I have a special assignment you asked me to go do tomorrow. I can't. My family member is dying. I've got to be there for my family.' That night, RJ had to work the midnight to 8:00 a.m. shift and still had to come the next day for the assignment. She said, 'We'll assign you to the hospital, that will be your post. You'll be there with your family. And don't worry about tomorrow, we'll find something for you.'" When RJ came back the next day, he was tasked to be the telephone operator for the day. "I was exhausted, so they kept me away from the event I needed to do (his original assignment). That is being flexible—the ability to maneuver your people around. With the respect that I got from her, my boss, it made me wanna be able to do whatever she needed me to do. If she asked me to go to a crappy assignment, no problem, I would do it because she did this for me," RJ said. "And that was from one of the toughest female bosses I've ever had!"

What Should Other Leaders Do? RJ said that a superior's attitude that "you are just a simple cop, a simple detective, and I am higher ranking than you, so you listen to what I say, because I don't care what you think" should be changed. RJ also said that some superiors think that being aggressive is a hallmark of good leadership. But he disagrees. "A good leader knows that he or she can be firm without being too aggressive." According to RJ, there is a huge distinction between "firm" and "aggressive." A good "firm" leader can implement strict adherence to rules and regulations, with as little deviation as possible, and still follow guidelines. But the domineering type of aggressive leader is one who can be extreme, whose actions border on the abuse of power. This is particularly evident when handing out disproportionately severe penalties for non-compliance.

Adherence to wearing the uniform properly is a strict requirement for law enforcers. In the New York City Police Department, taking away your basic vacation time is one of the ways to penalize an officer. "We would call that by its nickname term, 'rip.' You'd get a rip, say, if you got caught outside without your hat on. You could get a two-hour rip from your vacation time," RJ said. It was all within the power of the decision maker to hurt where it counted the most—take away precious vacation time from officers who needed it badly. "I had a boss who was really hard on this one guy. I don't know why he was, but he was just that—hard on him. The guy walked into the station house without his hat on, and he got a two-day rip; two days for not wearing his hat," RJ narrated. This is aggressive, according to RJ, almost an abuse of power.

RJ advises leaders to "remove personal feelings from work." It is key to quality leadership, he said. "We all know that some personalities just don't mesh; it's just normal." His advice to anyone in a leadership position whose personality clashes with a subordinate, is to leave all personal feelings at home. "Sometimes you can be a little too aggressive towards giving punishments when you see someone you do not like do something wrong. Be fair."

What If You Were on the Receiving End? "There was a situation where I had one boss, a 'he,' with whom I clashed every single day. I worked a different schedule than the rest of officers, because I was on special assignment. The majority of the precinct worked from 7:00 a.m. to 3:35 p.m. I started work at 9:30 a.m. and finished at 6:00 p.m. So, my schedule and my boss's were completely off. Every time I came into his office for attendance and said, 'Hey, I'm here,' this boss was in the middle of doing something. He would go ballistic! I then stormed off into my office. We just hated each other. One day, this whole idea of 'killing him with kindness' hit my mind. Before I came to work, I stopped and I got him coffee. I wrote a little ... note—scribbled the time I came in, what my tour was that day, and I taped it to the cup. I put the coffee on the big large desk that the lieutenant or sergeants used. The day I did that, I got into my office, and I received a phone call from him asking me, 'Did you spit in my coffee?' I'm like, 'No, I would not do that!' And he's like, 'All right. Thanks!' and hangs up the phone. I did it again the next day, every day for a whole week. He calls me up the day I didn't do it and said, 'Where's my coffee, man?' So, I came down, got some coffee, I came back, and we're sitting and chatting."

RJ, with this story, talked of how he had to consciously refocus his thoughts from feeling ignored to understanding his boss's situation, by starting with a breakthrough gesture of kindness. RJ said that he did not realize just how busy his boss was, and it might have been unfair to demand his attention. RJ refrained from thinking that he was more important than what his boss was doing. "We ended up being very good friends," he said. His boss learned from that experience too. He gave a subordinate he initially did not like very much a chance rather than be totally dismissive of him.

Women on the way to the top could be at the receiving end of personal biases, similar to what minorities may experience. That horror stories of discrimination exist cannot be denied, but stories of success abound, stories of how obstacles can be overcome. "That is why I say to any woman who wants to go after anything—anything at all—you should set your goals and get there. Use all those good examples from others, learn from them, and make them your own steps. Keep going because you can do it. You can do it," RJ promised.

Concluding Comments from Dr. Banez

In 1958, after Rosalind Elsie Franklin's death at age 37, her mentor, John Desmond Bernal (1901–1971), the well-known pioneer of using X-ray to elucidate atomic structures of molecules, spoke highly of Franklin's seminal work. Bernal noted, "her photographs were among the most beautiful X-ray photographs of any substance ever taken. Their excellence was the fruit of extreme care in preparation and mounting of the specimens, as well as in the taking of the photographs." Bernal was referring to Photograph 51. Franklin and her student, Raymond Gosling, made this now famous image using X-ray diffraction on the DNA molecule at King's College London, under physicist Sir John Turton Randall. Back in 1951, the structure of this all-important biomolecule, DNA, remained unknown. That is, until competing American scientists, James Watson and Francis Crick of the Cavendish Laboratory in Cambridge, who were also working on modeling the DNA structure, cracked the mystery by analyzing Photograph 51. But they did so without Franklin's participation, nor her permission, nor her knowledge that they were using her data and Photograph 51 retrieved from her drawer.

In 1962, James Watson, Francis Crick, and Maurice Wilkins (Sir J.T. Randall's deputy) were jointly awarded the Nobel Prize in Physiology and/or Medicine. Discovery of the double helix structure of DNA became forever associated with Watson and Crick. If you did not know Franklin's story of how her data was "borrowed" (hacked in today's jargon), or the lack of recognition for her major contribution to the discovery, you are not alone. Even women in science may have first read about Rosalind Franklin from James Watson's 1968 book, *The Double Helix: A Personal Account of the Discovery of the Double Helix Structure of DNA*. In that book, Watson's portrayal of Franklin's confrontational or harsh personality only matched his opinion of her appearance. Remembering his first glimpse of her at a conference in London in 1951, he wrote, "Momentarily I wondered how she would look if she took off her glasses and did something novel with her hair...."

Biographies written by Franklin's friend, Anne Sayre, in 1975, and by biographer Brenda Maddox in the 2002 book, *Rosalind Franklin: The Dark Lady of DNA*, refute the unflattering description of Franklin by James Watson. One characterization of her was that of an antisocial spinster. Twenty first century scientist, Ellen Elliot, drew inspiration from Maddox's book. In her blog post, *Women in Science: Remembering Rosalind Franklin, Why is it important to have women and minorities in STEM fields?* (Elliot, 2016), Elliot remarked, "very few people today know of her ground-breaking discoveries on the chemical structures of coal and graphite, or that she led the team that solved the 3D structure of the tomato mosaic virus (TMV). She was fascinated by viruses, and began studies on the polio virus shortly before her death. Franklin's publication record alone shows a scientist at the top of her field, with discoveries significant enough to have earned three Nobel Prizes."

"Although she never complained, Franklin dealt with her fair share of discrimination and sexism. As a woman and as a Jew, she often felt isolated from her colleagues, and these were challenges she was never quite able to overcome. As an undergraduate at Cambridge, she was denied the right to a Bachelor's Degree, as women were only entitled to the 'Degree Titular' at the time; Bachelor's Degrees were only granted to men. She also endured the Second World War while at Cambridge, and witnessed the British government caps on Jewish immigrants from Europe who were trying to escape Hitler's Third Reich. These restrictions enraged Franklin, and she found little sympathy at Cambridge."

Women's capacity for achievement at the highest levels of performance is beyond question. Take Marie Sklodowska (1867–1934), for example. She is better known by her married name, Marie Curie, and for being the first woman to win a Nobel Prize. But she won not one but two Nobel Prize awards in separate fields: one in 1903 in Physics for her and her husband Pierre's pioneering work in radioactivity, a term she coined. And in 1911, in Chemistry, for the discovery of radium and polonium as well as for creating a means to measure radioactivity. These discoveries advanced scientific knowledge and have many applications today, including use in cancer treatment and medicine. Yet in 1901, during the inception of her first Nobel Prize (awarded 1903), Marie was not even nominated. Credit for the work she did went exclusively to the male Curie, Pierre, her husband and scientific collaborator. Swedish mathematician Magnus Goesta Mittag-Leffler advocated for her inclusion because the French Academy of Science had originally nominated only Pierre and Henri Becquerel, the French physicist who discovered evidence of radioactivity before any other. The fact that Marie was female, a scientist of Polish ancestry, and working in a highly competitive field in Paris at the turn of the century may have had something to do with the initial snub. But any doubts as to her or any woman's ability to generate and examine ideas that lead to breakthrough scientific discoveries should be put to rest. As a mother, she nurtured Irene, her first daughter with Pierre, who together with her husband, also won the highest recognition in science—the 1935 Nobel Prize in Chemistry, for discovering artificial radioactivity.

A century later, it is tempting to state that progress has been made for women leading the fold in scientific quests, like Jane Goodall (born 1934). Openly criticized by other scientists for her unconventional methods—like assigning names to individual primates she studied—Goodall, nonetheless, continues to lead by hacking her own path, using her celebrity status, numerous awards, and huge mainstream following to forge her environmental advocacy. She was told that "scientists must be coldly objective and never show empathy for their subjects (i.e., chimpanzees)." However, she wrote in her 2018 *Time* magazine article, "*Dr. Jane Goodall: Being a Woman Was Crucial to My Success in a Male-Dominated Field*," that in fact, having empathy "can sometimes provide intuition about the meaning of a certain primate behavior." In this article, she stressed the need for women to have a collective voice and to unite, as captured in the following comments: "Because I succeeded in a scientific world largely dominated by men, I've been described as a feminist role model, but I never think of myself in that way. Although the feminist movement today is different, many women who have succeeded have done so by emphasizing their masculine characteristics. But we need feminine qualities to be both accepted and respected, and, in many countries, this is beginning to happen. I love that the new movement involves women joining their voices together on social media, thus giving a sense of solidarity."

Is it their tenacity and persistence, or maybe it is women's capacity to adapt to given conditions, resilience in the wake of rejection, as well as resourcefulness and creativity, that determined success for these women, whether recognized in their life time or not? Perhaps, it is their ability to become impervious to societal pressure to conform and their refusal to be boxed into assigned stereotypical roles and expectations that liberated women leaders from within. For women breaking away from the mold, handling personal attacks on looks and personality may be key. Many have paved the way by example. A woman's ascent to the number one position, however, requires skillful navigation of cultural hurdles—social constructs that institutionalize gender bias. Building alliances with other women can be productive. Note how successful women-led movements have become. Also, this period of high-speed technological leaps and global-scale socio-economic disruption of almost every aspect of modern life, as well as looming environmental threats and human (i.e., labor) displacement, can create shock and setbacks *or* they can manifest as opportunities. Through technology, women have the ability to shape the prevailing collective narrative about gender roles and leadership potential, band together, and communicate faster.

Paradox

In 2014, 2017, and again in 2018, *Harvard Business Review* published studies focused on female CEOs of Fortune 500 companies. In 2014, the article "Research: How Female CEOs Actually Get to Top" reported on a study that identified two conventional pieces of career advice for women aiming for the top post: "(1) get an undergraduate degree from the most prestigious school you can, an MBA from a selective business school, then (2) land a job at a top consulting firm or investment bank." However, authors Sarah Dillard and Vanessa Lipschitz concluded that "female CEOs didn't have to go to the best schools or get the most prestigious jobs. But they did have to find a good place to climb."

In 2017, *Harvard Business Review* authors Jane Edison Stevenson and Evelyn Orr wrote an article titled "We Interviewed 57 Female CEOs to Find Out How More Women Can Get to the Top." Only 6.4 percent of Fortune 500 companies, according to them, were run by female CEOs. They interviewed other women CEOs outside the top 500. They noted that 32, the number of Fortune 500 female CEOs that year, was the highest ever, a jump of 21 from the previous year. They then suggested actions for companies to take to build a pipeline for female CEOs.

In 2018, the *Harvard Business Review* article titled "How Women Manage the Gendered Norms of Leadership," authors Wei Zheng, Ronit Kark, and Alyson Meister described the situation for women leaders as a "Catch 22." They wrote that in business, like in society, female leaders are required to be "nice and warm" because those qualities are traditionally expected of women in general. This concept of a woman being "nice and warm" may simply be a cultural construct. But in business, female leaders are also expected to be "competent or tough" because the society as a whole expects "competent or tough" from men and from leaders. These qualities can be viewed as opposites, or mutually exclusive. Unfortunately, that view can put women leaders in a double bind because they are expected to be both. By default, society imagines leaders to be male. As such, a "ruling female" is the exception. So, the "queen" needs to be "nice and warm" and "competent or tough" even more so than any male counterpart to be considered successful.

"Competent or Tough"

No enterprise could be tougher than the business of defense and policing. How do women leaders fare in testosterone-driven, hierarchical, and violence-prone environments? No woman has been president of the United States, so there has been no female commander-in-chief in this country to date. Since the first U.S. Secretary of Defense James Forrestal's appointment in 1947 to the present, 27 secretaries later, no appointee has ever been female. Only men have served as secretary of the U.S. Department of Justice, the executive branch responsible for law enforcement at the federal level, although, Janet Reno served as Attorney General during President Clinton's administration.

The Federal Bureau of Investigation (FBI) reported that in 2017, 12.5 percent of all officers in the police force nationwide were female. Women have served as chiefs of police, the highest rank in law enforcement. According to Phil Keith, Director of the COPS Office of the U.S. Department of Justice, 300 police chiefs in the country are women (2019). Appointed chief of the Portland Police Bureau in 1985, Penny Harrington became the first female ever to head a major police department in the U.S. She resigned in 1986, a year later, and in 1987 filed a suit claiming that members of the department "conspired to embarrass and drive her from office." In 1994, Beverly Harvard's appointment as Atlanta's chief of police was confirmed by the City Council after she served as the acting chief for six months. Harvard became the country's first female African American police chief.

After serving for eight years, she decided not to reapply for the job in 2002, but stayed in the force. Three years after her appointment in 2016 as Portsmouth police chief, Tonya Chapman, the first black woman in Virginia to hold this post, told the press that she was forced out in March 2019. She said, "some quite frankly did not like taking directions from an African-American female." The complicated race relations in Virginia at this time may have also played a significant role in the dynamics among her department, community, and politics.

What do male insiders say? Retired officer RJ noted the need for women leaders in a male-dominated paramilitary organization like NYPD to walk a tightrope. On the one hand, women superiors cannot be overbearing, but on the other, cannot be so tough as to be completely inflexible and perceived as abusive of power. RJ qualified the meaning of overbearing as "over-mothering" or "too-nurturing." Said another way, Sheriff's Deputy Robert alluded to micromanaging as a question of trust. He added that it feels as if male subordinates in a hierarchical structure are reminded of being nagged to clean their bedrooms, something they dislike. By their admission, however, men in the force respected women who needed to pass the same physical and knowledge competencies required of men for both entry level and leadership positions. And they also value women's person-to-person communication skills and see it as an advantage when navigating tricky human interactions in the field and in politics. Thus, it appears that all the elements for effective leadership are in place. But it is the right blend or balance between "nice and warm" and "competent or tough" that determines longevity in the top position. Both RJ and Robert have seen changes in the cultural attitude towards women leaders within the force. They both express optimism in women's ascent to the highest rank when an institutional support system is in place.

From Chief to Chef

How about women in industries traditionally associated within the "nice and warm," for example, women employed in the hospitality industry? Do women have it easier climbing career ladders in service-oriented businesses that mirror the customary role for women in the domestic realm, like cooking? Shouldn't the top positions in the food service industry be crowded with women? In 2017, the number of male chefs and head cooks in the U.S. numbered 340,000, while 95,000 (or 21.9 percent) made up the female workforce, according to Data USA, a free platform that allows users to access shared government data. Analyzing the U.S. Bureau of Statistics data of the 2017 median weekly earnings of full-time salaried chefs and head cooks, the *Narrow the Gap* website posted that "women chefs and head cooks make 78 cents to the dollar men earn doing the same job." According to the website, "that's $141 out of a weekly paycheck, which means she (a woman who is a chef and head cook) gets paid, $7,332 less per year." "Equal pay for equal work" could very well be the institutional support that aspiring women leaders need for additional motivation. Until conditions change, however, what are aspirants to do in an industry that is as competitive, if not more cutthroat, than any other?

Based on Rosemarie's experience and what she recalled, operations at all levels of management and categories of food service (fast, casual, fine, and hotel) have traditionally been dominated by women. However, men occupied the very top positions, like executive chef and financial management-related posts. Every time Rosemarie rose in rank, moved to a bigger corporation or switched categories in the industry, she dealt with becoming boss to a previous male supervisor or one who had more experience with the company but less training. Her people skills-set, one that allowed her to acknowledge that excellent interpersonal and communication skills were part of her strength as a woman, came in handy. She understood the male ego, having had male siblings, and knew how to effectively deal with men. Her self-confidence and competencies helped her turn male-female relationship challenges into opportunities. Engaging men in healthy collaborations led to lasting and productive professional connections.

Many propose explanations as to why men dominate top positions in professional kitchens. One reason cited is that the gender gap reflects the wider society's bias. Cultural perceptions, say for example, that "chefs are male and white," matter in the restaurant business because an investor's vision of success attracts capital. Differences in their approach to cooking—men are more innovative or experimental versus women are traditional and nurturing—may also hold water. But the 2019 blog post "Why are there so few female chefs—the gender balance in the Culinary Industry" by Chefify also mentioned that women become parents earlier than men, right around the crucial stage of career development. Women remain the family's primary caregiver. Thus, the movement from a home cooking job, a gender-based role for women in the domestic realm, to a professional cooking career should be quite an easy leap. Women's labor at home and her experience with domestic work have never been given monetary value in the economic sense.

In 2016, Swedish author Katrine Marcal wrote the book *Who Cooked Adam Smith's Dinner?* In it, she questioned a well-established idea of Adam Smith's, who is considered the "Father of Economics," that self-interest drives human actions. Smith described the "economic man" as motivated by financial gains, which in turn powered the economic scene. Marcal pointed out that the work women do at home as an actual contribution to the economy was totally absent in Smith's economic model of the free market. According to Marcal, men are able to act in self-interest, because women (mothers, wives, daughters, and sisters) care for children, cook dinner, and clean house without compensation. It is not surprising then that in the business realm, women in leadership positions are expected to balance career with gender-based domestic roles. A female CEO must meet expectations (of being "nice and warm" and more competent than anyone else) and also bear the cost of "nurturing" her family on less compensation than her male counterpart, who is relatively free from domestic obligations, assumed to act in self-interest, and made to believe he is superior.

Professional Caregiver

How about the nurturing profession? This conundrum should not happen in the nursing profession. The business of caring for the sick, having been professionalized by a woman, is still female-dominated. In 2013, the U.S. Census Bureau Newsroom reported findings of the study *Men in Nursing Occupations.* The percentage of male registered nurses increased from 2.7 percent in 1970 to 9.6 percent in 2011 in the U.S. Although 90 percent of the nursing workforce is female, nursing executives are not always women. In 2017, Halle Tecco, Founder Emeritus of Rock Health, a venture fund dedicated to digital health, wrote, "the most common hospital executive role for women leaders is Chief Nursing Officer, of which 60% are women." In the healthcare industry, overall, 46 percent of the workforce is female. Yet according to Rock Health's analysis of U.S. Bureau of Statistics data, "on average, they (women) still spend more than twice as much time caring for and helping household members. Women also bear a disproportionate burden of informal caregiving for family members, friends, neighbors, serving as 66% of all caregivers (the estimated value of said informal care is over $148B)." Tecco (2017) reported that 22.6 percent of Fortune 500 companies in healthcare had women in the vice president, president, and chief positions. No Fortune 500 healthcare company, however, had a female CEO in 2017.

It would be easy to assume that a male-female salary gap does not exist in the female dominated nursing profession. But gender wage gaps do exist. "Salary Differences Between Male and Female Registered Nurses in the United States," a Research Letter published in 2015 by the *Journal of American Medical Association (JAMA)*, reported that a survey analysis showed men's salaries (unadjusted for demographic and other factors) were higher than women nurses' salaries. Although the difference is not statistically significant over time (six years of the survey period), regression analysis showed the estimated overall gap in adjusted earnings to be $5,148.

M. Brian, a male nurse who spent 10 year on a nighttime shift in the Intensive Care Unit (ICU) of a big hospital in Miami, saw women nursing chiefs come and go. As a nurse, he singled out the part that he enjoyed most about the job—caring for patients and assuring families that their loved ones are cared for. This, to M. Brian, is the tightrope that women in leadership roles need to navigate. The must balance the demands of the business side of health care, such as making money for shareholders and keeping profit numbers up, while at the same time motivating and empowering workers to provide excellent and compassionate care. Most health care workers are committed to helping others and enjoy what they do, or they would not be in this job in the first place.

Having worked two nursing jobs (two eight-hour shifts) for more than 20 years, nurse E. Barrido knew exactly what commitment and satisfaction from providing care meant. As she pared down the number of assisted and special care facilities she owned back to the few she started with, she emphasized that she could have made millions more in earnings. On the other hand, she mused that had she cheated her employees of their pay, or simply not cared for their well-being, her business may not even be around now. Instead, it lasted and prospered because she invested in making her employees' jobs enjoyable. To her, profit flowed from the excellent service provided by happy, satisfied health care workers. Work that involved decisions and action that had life or death implications required kindness and compassion. It also called for integrity and precision. To Barrido, it is crystal clear that human capital is the core business in nursing care.

Also rising to the nursing executive position in a busy New York City hospital, Ces Lim, an immigrant, a wife, and a mother, knew first-hand the pressure to keep labor costs down. But as a mother, out-of-schedule requests for time off can tug at her heartstrings. Substitute nurses or overtime pay for other staff to cover for others' absence cost money. Yet like fathers, nurses who are mothers want to attend their kids' baseball games and recitals. They also need to leave on the dot to keep their kids from waiting for after school pick-up. Graduate school classes, professional meetings, and training sessions outside of work hours—opportunities that could lead to promotions down the road—take a back seat to childcare at every stage of a child's growth. In fact, Lim had heard refusals to offers of promotion, or requests to be considered at a later time, from mothers still raising children. Lim considered herself lucky to have an extended family. She forged ahead and took opportunities to study and advance her career because her mother took care of her daughter. Her supportive husband, also busy with his career, understood why she was not home to cook dinner for the family, and why she worked on holidays. Having gone through a similar experience, 2020 Democratic presidential candidate, Senator Elizabeth Warren, thanked her Aunt Bee who came to live with her family to care for her kids, because without her support, she could not have continued teaching in law school back in the 1970s-1980s.

Deputy Mayor and City Administrator of the City of St. Petersburg in Florida, Dr. Kanika Tomalin was a hospital executive who knew about profit, service, and being a woman leader. Early success as a journalist for a major local newspaper motivated Dr. Tomalin to aspire to become part of the leadership team. This meant learning the inner workings of the management team that looked at the bottom line. Experience on the business side of publishing prepared her for policy work in health care and eventually city administration. When asked to comment on women and leadership, Dr. Tomalin said that she certainly sees the value in subscribing to two schools of thought on woman and successful leadership. One: the school that ignores gender as a factor in good leadership and marginalizes any contribution that being a woman plays in successful leadership; and the other: which totally embraces womanhood as the central focus of women as leaders, taking full advantage of the nurturing nature of women. The sweet spot must be somewhere in between. When asked to clarify what "being a woman" means, Dr. Tomalin explained that "the mysticism in the alchemy of walking in this life as a woman defies articulation. But the chemistry is in knowing that being a woman allows for nurturing and that knowledge transcends time and space."

CHAPTER 6

Let's Hear It from the Millennials

An Accidental Discovery

A FORTUITOUS COMBINATION OF SHEER LUCK and coincidence sometimes are all it takes for accidental discoveries to change the course of history. For instance, let's consider the chance discovery of the first antibiotic, penicillin, in 1929. According to an article on inventions that changed the world by Melissa Breyer (*Ten Accidental Inventions that Changed the World*, 2013), this chance discovery "happened in 1929 when a young bacteriologist, Sir Alexander Fleming, was tidying up his lab. After having been on vacation, he returned to work to find that a petri dish of Staphylococcus bacteria had been left uncovered; and he noticed that the mold on the culture had killed many of the bacteria. He identified the mold as *penicillium notatum*, and upon further research found that it could kill other bacteria and could be given to small animals without ill effect."

Another chance discovery that liberated housewives from the drudgery of cooking for long hours is the indispensable microwave. For someone who is cooking-impaired and finds no satisfaction in cooking and other household chores, this timesaver device brought me sanity, discretionary time to be creative, and the luxury of not using my conventional oven. When friends visit, they are amazed at how spectacularly clean and spotless my KitchenAid oven is. I don't tell them that I only use it at Thanksgiving, once a year, to roast the turkey. Other than a single day in November, it remains unused, undisturbed, and immaculate.

Since most great discoveries and innovations happen by accident, it's important to spot this serendipitous event as an opportunity to further explore the original idea—like this unexpected detour on the topic of women and power from the perspective of Millennials. During my interviews with powerful women, I noticed that Millennials and Gen Xers, closest in age to Millennials, have a distinct and unique relationship with power. They appear to be comfortable with exercising power, and it seems to be part and parcel of who they are. It's a healthy and natural relationship that's an integral part of the Millennials' zeitgeist, an emerging spirit that's slowly defining this generation. It makes me wonder how this transformation happened. Can I attribute this coming of age to the socialization and experience provided by their Gen X parents? Is this *tribal knowledge* a net gain from decades of learning and knowledge transmitted by Gen X parents and other individuals open to change? Of course, these are initial impressions that need to be validated by more solid data through intensive research, possibly the subject of another publication.

I first noticed this positive movement when I interviewed Deputy Secretary Courtney Stewart, who impressed me with the way she wields power and leads employees with such grace, elegance, and spontaneity. The ability to lead and influence the behavior of others comes naturally to her. It's part of her psyche and who she is. Self-leadership, power, and influence are part of her behavioral make-up. I pursued this germ of an idea by conversing with other Millennials that I encountered in workplaces, at meetings, and at conferences. They appear to have a similar, if not the same, relationship with power. It comes naturally to them; it's almost ingrained and intrinsic to who they are. When I asked them about challenges they might have encountered in the workplace as women leaders, they were silent and were a bit lost as to how to respond to my question. I observed the same self-confidence, self-leadership, and natural ability to influence others when I attended the Annual Millennial Summit at the Chase Center in Wilmington, Delaware. I attended the workshop on *Bridging the Divide: Cross-Generational Mentoring,* and just sat there, observed, and delighted in the participants' vibrant discussion. The Millennials in attendance gave me the impression that they prefer mentoring from their peers as opposed to coaching from other experienced leaders from other generational cohorts. Millennials work to live, not live to work. Work is simply a means to an end, although they are looking for meaningful work and innovation, which at face value appears to be a contradiction. Despite subscribing to the utilitarian value of work, they prefer to have work that is creative and meaningful. Is this mindset an extension of their worldview on life? After this event, I decided to further pursue this topic by conducting a focus group on women and power from the perspective of today's Millennials.

The Millennials or Echo Boomers: The Next Great Generation of Leaders

As an organizational consultant and an executive coach, I've had the good fortune of working with exceptional women leaders representing different generational demographic cohorts, such as the Baby Boomer (born between 1946 and 1964) and the Millennial generations. The Pew Research Center defines Millennials as the demographic cohort born between 1981 to 1996, while authors-demographers William Strauss and Neil Howe proposed start and end dates of 1982 to 2004. A report published in 2017 by the U.S. Census Bureau noted that "there really isn't an official start and end date for when Millennials were born." This demographic cohort represents a majority of the women that I have had the opportunity to interact with and coach or mentor in the workplace. The women who participated in the focus group are Millennials, also known as Echo Boomers because they are the offspring of Baby Boomers, and they were also born during a period of high birth rates (1980 through the mid–1990s).

The Millennials are currently the largest demographic cohort in the American labor force. Research conducted by the Pew Research Center reported that "as of 2017—the most recent year for which data are available—56 million Millennials (those ages 21 to 36 in 2017) were working or looking for work. There were more than the 53 million Generation Xers, who accounted for a third of the labor force. And it was well ahead of the 41 million Baby Boomers, who represented a quarter of the total. Millennials surpassed Gen Xers in 2016." It's important to understand this generation, because they are the leaders and workers who will be shaping the future of this country. Below is a sampling of the attributes, core values, and competencies of Millennials (Pew Research Center, WMFC 2019 Generational Differences Chart, & William Strauss and Neil Howe) shaping today's workplace:

- Millennials are looking for **meaningful work** and **innovation**: According to the 2013 Millennial Impact Report conducted by Achieve Agency (funded by the Case Foundation), Millennials are in search of jobs that provide their lives meaning and purpose, that is, jobs that allow them to make a contribution to the lives of others.

- Millennials and **social justice**: They intend to make a difference in the world by supporting a worthy cause of their choice, being active in advocating for their favorite charity or nonprofit organizations, and doing volunteer work in support of their missions and programs. The report noted that 83 percent of the Millennials who participated in the survey donated to a charity of their choice. It also reported that "Millennials view volunteer opportunities as a way to socially connect with like-minded peers, which moves them beyond technology (social networking) to in-person action." It concluded that networking activities "maximize their inherent social connectedness," while performing a function that they value and enjoy.

- Millennials and **work-life balance**: They work to live, and work is simply a means to an end. They not only balance the demands of work, family, and a quality life, but they also make time for community development and self-development. Flexible working hours, job sharing, and telecommuting are important considerations for this demographic group.

- Millennials are **digital natives**: They are tech-savvy because technology, social media, and a networked global world have always been an integral part of their lives. They use technology to implement changes in the workplace, and they are aware and comfortable with change as a constant factor in a technology-powered information society.

- Millennials are great **communicators** and need constant and open communications: They use emails, cell phones, instant messaging, and text to communicate efficiently and effectively. If the message is important, they prefer in-person communication and expect clarity in work goals and expectations.
- Millennials work well in a **team environment**, not in a hierarchical structure: They believe in supporting others, in seeking different perspectives, and leading from any position. They thrive in a collaborative work environment because they have been socialized from a young age to participate with their Boomer parents to make decisions about areas that affect their lives, such as choices in terms of what sports to play, where to go for family vacations, and colleges to consider for further education. They have actively participated in teams from pre-school through college, so teamwork is part of their early socialization into adult society.
- Millennials are **task-oriented**: Results are important to them, no matter how long it takes to achieve the desired outcomes. Performance evaluations and rewards are important to them.

Focus Group Findings: The Great Reveal

Listening to the Millennials' lively and vibrant discussion was much like sipping a cool, refreshing drink from an ancient spring. The encounter reenergized my battered spirit and brought me new found hope that there might be movement in our struggle for workplace parity and power and inspired me to forge ahead.

On August 12, 2019, I invited ten women to participate in a focus group to further explore the views and perceptions of Millennials on women and power. They came from all three counties in Delaware, were between the ages of 24 to 42, and represented a diversity of careers and professions. There was a professor-consultant, a nurse navigator, a policy director, an HR professional, two AmeriCorps VISTA (Volunteers in Service to America), a dentist, two librarians, and a small business owner (farm). Eight of the ten participants were Millennials, while two were at the cusp of the Gen X-Millennial generations. I posed six questions to the participants, which covered the following themes:

- Character traits and key qualities to gain and keep power
- Eight competencies to gain and keep power
- Positive experiences and challenges about women, power, and the workplace
- How to best assist women to achieve parity in power and influence
- Attitudes or behaviors women need to change to gain and keep power
- Major differences between Millennials and the previous generations in handling/managing power

On Character

Much like the remarkable women that I interviewed in Chapter 4, the Millennials also affirmed the importance of the four quadrants in my WomenPower Paradigm on Character. They realize the importance of self-knowledge, doing for others, and doing for the common good, when wielding and using power. One major difference is that they don't appear to subscribe to a universal "Truth," but rather appear to value a more "subjective representation of the truth." What emerged in the short discussion is a version of the "Truth" that's presented more like a conviction, a belief, where there are wide gray areas open to individual interpretations of what's right or wrong. The HR specialist remarked that "self-knowledge is the most important quality. Knowing yourself will allow a woman in power to maintain boundaries and not be improperly influenced or be taken advantage of. Self-knowledge empowers women in power to use their voice to lead and guide others, as well as maintain respect from others." The professor noted that "knowing yourself enables you to identify areas where you excel, as well as areas for growth. Honesty, integrity, and courage are keys to helping you stand firm in the wave of controversy." One of the librarians echoed a similar sentiment: "self-knowledge is key; you must be comfortable and confident in yourself to effectively lead others." The HR specialist pointed out that "power should be shared." The dentist concluded that "all of the traits (listed in the wheel on character) have something in common—they indicate that our purpose is really in helping others. We do that by not only understanding ourselves, but also others in society. When we use our talents and knowledge to benefit society, we elevate not only society but ourselves." Below are some of the character traits mentioned by the participants, which are mostly *personal traits and values:*

- Others can be fearful or shy, so be relatable, real, and approachable
- Fearlessness
- Be firm with challenges
- Empathy
- All are connected/linked
- Openness
- To change others' opinions
- Know your truths but might not be able to fix [problem]
- Mental mindset
- Even playing field with someone more powerful
- Being hardworking and determined are most important traits
- Trusting instinct
- Know how to manipulate power
- Have something/resources that people need
- Power versus control
- Fear is stronger than hope
- We don't learn from history—definition of insanity

On Competencies

I feel validated using a modified focus group process since it appears to have paid off when I posed the question concerning recommended competencies. In addition to having a free-flowing conversation on the eight recommended professional competencies, I also asked the group to list and capture their perceptions and opinions on the survey form that I distributed to complement the discussion. Now, I have three sources of live, vivid, and clear data—the focus group discussion (which was captured in writing by Katie McDonough, administrative librarian from the Delaware Division of Libraries), the written comments to the questions, and the taped conversation. In the majority, the participants were in agreement with the suggested competencies and validated the importance of each competency with a lively discussion on the topics. Here are some of the comments from the group:

- All eight competencies are very important.
- All of these competencies allow for a more confident and self-aware person.
- Each of these is critical to success. Political skills may be the most helpful, in addition to financial acumen. Understanding how a business succeeds, profit and loss, etc., are critical to gaining respect as a leader.
- Communication skills are very important to be able to keep power. Management, leadership, and people skills are also important. As decisions and problems occur, a strong woman leader needs to have problem-solving and decision-making skills. Effective communication skills: all women [leaders need to be able] to communicate with a variety of personalities in the workplace.
- Add financial acumen.
- Teamwork: vital for the majority of careers. Companies that work together are often more efficient and are more harmonious. Teamwork+Harmony=Efficiency=Success!

The only competency that was not discussed or even mentioned was conflict resolution. In essence, this competency could be a

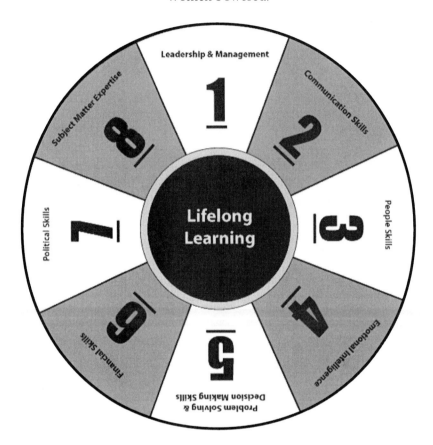

Figure 7: Core Competencies of Powerful Women–Revised WomenPower Paradigm

component of problem-solving skills. So, we revised the Competency Skills and replaced conflict resolution with Financial and Business Skills (#6) as a desired competency, as reflected in the graphics above.

Work Hacks: The group also suggested some key traits and practices that powerful women in leadership roles might consider adopting. We call them *Work Hacks*, simple, common-sense, and tested methods or techniques to increase efficiency and success in the workplace. They are comparable to life hacks.

- Don't work harder; work smarter.
- Know the ins and outs of a job.

- Don't be intimidating, [practice] humility and gratitude, and say "thank you!"
- People who ask questions want to do the job right.
- Market your business and yourself.
- [Do] outreach, networking.
- Self-promotion versus self-absorption.
- Be authentic.
- Have common sense.
- Relationship development.

The Millennial Divide: Are You an Old Millennial or a Young Millennial?

There was an interesting discussion on what a Millennial is and what period it covers. Some of the participants claimed that although they were born within the date range of the Millennial cohorts (1981–1996, according to the Pew Research Center), they don't feel like the technology-possessed, social-media obsessed, young Millennials. Dr. Jean Twenge, an American psychologist who has done extensive research on this generational cohort, explores the reasons why the young Millennials (born between 1986 and 2000), what she calls "Generation Me," are "tolerant, confident, open-minded, and ambitious but also disengaged, narcissistic, distrustful, and anxious." There is an emerging body of evidence that might explain why there's a dichotomy in patterns of beliefs, values, and behaviors between these two cohorts. The old Millennials, who were born between the early eighties and 1986, have gone through different historical periods. These older Millennials were *young adults* when the financial crisis of 2008 hit the economic scene. Some were graduating from college but many were already employed. This catastrophic financial debacle appears to have affected the career choices of the old Millennials, who assumed the traditional career paths of their Gen X and Baby Boomer parents (*Are You an Old Millennial or a Young Millennial?* 2019, CNN Report). In contrast, the crisis affected Young Millennials during their formative years, which made them more realistic and more practical. Twenge cites evidence from survey data that indicates that this group is less idealistic than Old Millennials and "they are more attracted to industries with steady work and are more likely to say that they are willing to work overtime."

Another key milestone that affected the younger Millennials was the introduction of the smartphones in 2007, when Apple unveiled the iPhone, Microsoft introduced the Windows Phone, and Google offered the Android. In essence, the younger Millennials were digital natives and were born and raised in a world where technology and instant communication were inherent fixtures of their brave new world. Compare this with the older Millennials who didn't get smartphones until their twenties. They were familiar with landlines, touch-tones, and rotary phones. Although Twenge concedes that there's not ample data on this subject as of now, this technological innovation affected how Millennials communicate. Young Millennials prefer to send a text or send an email, rather than use the telephone.

How do these differences in worldview and the manner in which these two groups communicate affect their relationship to power? A handful of articles on the topic indicate that Millennials prefer to work in a flat organization rather than a top-down, hierarchical workplace, which is called *Holacracy*. Marshall Hargrave (*What is Holacracy?* July 6, 2019) defined *Holacracy* as a "system of corporate governance whereby members of a team or business form distinct, autonomous, yet symbiotic teams to accomplish tasks and company goals. The concept of corporate hierarchy is discarded in favor of a flat organizational structure where all workers have an equal voice while simultaneously answering to the direction of a shared authority." Does this type of organizational structure encourage individuals to exercise greater self-leadership and empowerment? How does it influence their relationship to power? These are questions that could only be answered by more extensive research on this specific topic. Although there isn't enough solid empirical evidence to validate this claim, it appears that Millennials profiled in this book handle power with greater ease, comfort, and confidence than the earlier generations.

Positive Experiences and Challenges
Experienced by Women in the Workplace

The HR Specialist remarked that a positive example would be a woman who is able to harmoniously balance the demands of work with the demands of life and family. She noted that "a woman with power who can lead, work hard, can breathe, can have fun, takes time for family or personal interests, etc." is a model that most women might choose to aspire to. She proclaimed that *"women can't have it all! It is a challenge* to try to be a superwoman," which the rest of the group supported loudly and enthusiastically. The policy director chimed in, "I have a group of female colleagues and peers who have been incredibly supportive. This network of peers serves as a place to vent or process challenges and cheers to success." The librarian confessed that "women are strong, smart, powerful, and can reach goals that they put their minds to." However, she observed that even in female-dominated industries, males are still getting paid more. One of the VISTAs agreed and added that at times there is a "power struggle dynamic between women." As I have stated several times in this book, the only way for women to triumph is if we support each other in this challenging endeavor. Changing systems and culture is a complex and dynamic task that requires a collective effort. The other librarian confessed that "I appreciate managers and supervisors who listen to and value the knowledge and experience of their employees. I've had multiple female supervisors who excel at this." She confessed that it can be a challenge for women leaders to at times "balance being likeable and being respected." Her revealing comment is indicative of the changing leadership landscape for women in the workplace. The ability to wield and keep power among women is not a monolithic experience—there are clusters of positive movement and growth. The professor concluded that "Women in power I've worked for who made a positive impact on me were committed to taking me under their wings. They allowed me to shadow them in meetings, take on responsibilities, and helped me network with others in power around the organization." This is precisely the type of leadership that we're trying to learn, adopt, and master.

Other challenges that the group listed include the following: work life balance; women without kids tend to have more power; man-made social norms; jealousy; not a workaholic mentality; breastfeeding; pressure to have it all; and lack of self-confidence.

Suggestions on How to Achieve Parity in Power and Influence

The librarian listed crucial steps that women can take to improve their chances of success, such as: support one another and advocate for other women leaders; put less pressure on yourself and others and be proud and supportive of each other; knowledge-sharing; and don't be afraid to get in the trenches with employees. Such wise words of wisdom from one so young! The HR specialist expressed similar sentiments, with words of wisdom, such as "encouragement and support to do things differently and to embrace individuality." She pointed out that "there's a societal norm for women about how they should live, work, and the goals they should have. If we can give ourselves and others the permission to break the mold and societal expectations," maybe we can achieve greater parity in the workplace. Other well-thought-out suggestions include the following: amplify your voices; practice empathy; speak up to injustices; be kind; empower other women; be compassionate; do things differently; don't ask staff to do things you wouldn't do; and listen to feedback.

Attitudes and Behaviors to Change

When I posed this question, one of the participants asked "why do women have to be the ones to change?" She's on target! To improve the power inequality in the workplace, both players have to work together to address the key problems and find a balanced solution that benefits all. The majority of the women touched on the value of flexibility and change. Here is a sample of the comments on these complementary ideas: fight for flexibility, and be willing to change the paradigm; be flexible and open to something different; flexibility is not a bad thing; times are changing—something different is coming; and change the fact that women have to do things a certain way, be a certain way, or have a certain amount of experience—be open to something different.

Major Differences Among Millennials, Baby Boomers, and Generation X

Here are some of the insightful comments from the group on the differences between Millennials and the two generations preceding them:

- Technology is a huge difference. We are more comfortable with technology, which helps to make our lives easier but also more complex. For example, I can order my groceries online, but I also have a million platforms to check, and I need to be accessible constantly.
- We work to live, not live to work!
- Boomers: Live to work; loyalty to job; trouble adapting to technology. Millennials: Work to live; focused on happiness and self-actualization; our jobs don't necessarily allow for loyalty (unstable job market); more comfortable with technology but we can get information overload; need more hand holding.
- Older generations of women in power just do what's necessary to get by and sustain what level of power they do have. Whereas, younger generations of women have confidence to take risks, build relationships, and take different approaches to catapult the power they have.
- Previous generations don't always see our generation as hard working, and younger generations feel that older generations allowed themselves to not have a voice and be walked over. Life is easier for us [Millennials].

CHAPTER 7

Conclusions
and Path Forward

THE FINDINGS AND INSIGHTS PRESENTED BELOW are tentative conclusions and observations based on the current study.

Gender Stratification Is a
Culturally-Imposed Norm

Here's a simple but profound truth: *The dominance of men over women is a culturally-imposed norm that has no scientific, biological, or genetic basis.* It is a gender stratification that has been artificially-imposed and sanctioned by an imperfect society for hundreds of years. This is a myth that needs to be summarily debunked. Recent studies (Gallup Survey, 2015; Victor Lipman, 2015) have, in fact, confirmed that women are as capable as men as leaders and managers.

Social norms are culturally-specific ways that we're *expected to behave* and are imposed on us by other members of society. Norms affect every aspect of our lives and, many times, we adhere to and follow norms without even thinking about them. We have been socialized to behave in such a way that we're not even aware of it. It's important to remember that social norms *change* over time, like the historical period when the American public valued racial segregation in schools because society rejected the concept of racial equality. Not so long ago, women were traditionally relegated to staying home as homemakers and could not have had careers of their own. The workplace was no place for a woman to be. A majority of society

158

conformed to this social norm until the advent of the women's movement, when women revolted against this cultural norm that subjugated their freedom of choice. There were no laws that sanctioned this status; it was simply a way of maintaining order in a society that allowed men to effectively control behavior. *Leadership, power, and influence are learned behaviors that can be improved, nurtured, and honed through systematic learning and experience.*

Impressionistic and Fragmentary

The findings of this limited qualitative research do not have the controls and precision of a scientifically-validated research, and as such, generalizations apply only to the population discussed in this present study. We are not assuming that all women of all ages, cultures, racial, educational, and political affiliations form a homogeneous group. We're simply presenting the findings and insights in this book as a first-step towards the intentional and systematic training and coaching of women to gain and keep power.

Carpe the Chaos: The Opportunity Side of Change

Confusion is good; chaos is a good. When the rules of the game are changing and boundaries are moving and becoming penetrable, opportunities to introduce new ways of thinking and behaving are maximized. These transitions present golden opportunities for cultural change, when norms are in question and new patterns of behavior, beliefs, and values are emerging. Old paradigms are displaced by new paradigms. We are at this juncture in the evolution of women and power, as can be gleaned from the focus group findings on the Millennials' perspectives on power in Chapter 6. Let's seize the moment!

I immigrated to this country (Delaware, USA) from the Philippines in 1967, at exactly the precise historical period when Delaware and fifteen other states saw their anti-miscegenation laws over-turned by the passage of the *Loving v. Virginia* ruling by the United State Supreme Court. This civil rights victory decriminalized inter-marriage between racial groups. My Filipino friend, who attempted to get married to his Caucasian fiancée in the early 1960s, could not get a marriage license because marriages between whites and Fili-pinos were illegal at that time. They had to move the wedding to the District of Columbia, where it was legal to be married to someone from a different racial group. Despite the passage of the Civil Rights Act of 1964, it wasn't until three years later that Delaware and fifteen other states were forced to accept interracial marriages as legal.

In 2019, close to six decades later, there appears to be an increase in interracial marriages in the United States, from 3 percent in 1967 to 17 percent in 2015 (Pew Research Center, May 2017). In Delaware, I suspect several factors contributed to the greater acceptance of mixed marriages, such as increased immigration of Asians and His-panics, the presence of Dover Air Force Base, higher educational lev-els, and changing attitudes towards minorities. All contributed to this changing paradigm. These are simply assumptions that need to be validated by empirical data, which is beyond the scope of this cur-rent research. However, the key point in this discussion is that when paradigms are shifting, people's perspectives and beliefs are funda-mentally altered and new trails to the future are wide open—oppor-tunities abound. Let's seize the moment, build on the momentum created by pioneers, and systematically ensure the ascent of women into positions of leadership and power. This monumental task could only be achieved through collective, intentional, sustained, and stra-tegic efforts.

Situational Leadership and Servant Leadership

It appears that a majority of the female leaders we interviewed were successful because they adopted situational leadership styles, combined with servant leadership, in their organizations and other spheres of influence. There is increasing evidence that effective and powerful leaders employ situational leadership styles in managing and leading organizations. An in-depth discussion of situational leadership is on page 44, while additional comments on servant leadership are on page 51.

Alignment with the WomenPower Model

Overall, evidence seems to affirm that the female leaders' assessment of how to gain and keep power is in congruence with the WomenPower Paradigm. There were only two suggested modifications, that came from Congresswoman Lisa Blunt Rochester and Deputy Director Beth-Ann Ryan. Lisa expressed a strong opinion on the inclusion of *lifelong learning* as a competency that needs to be part of the model. Beth-Ann Ryan also suggested that "personal traits, such as self-confidence, flexibility, being collaborative, tenacity, and persistence are crucial in gaining and keeping power." For example, she added, "men appear to have greater self-confidence than women ... or maybe, they're better at faking it. Women are raised and taught to be quiet, to listen, to be polite, and not to take over meetings." We agreed that men are socialized to be self-assured and to lead, while women are raised to be sensitive to others and to be supportive rather than assertive. Another modification suggested by the focus group participants is the inclusion of *financial skills* as a key component of the competency model.

Systematic Process: Intentional, Deliberate, and Collective

As we have stated and stressed throughout this book, the only way to acquire and keep power is to be ***intentional and deliberate*** and to stay focused on the prize. The other critical ingredient in this journey of transformation and change is that it demands a ***collective effort***. This individual and systems change requires an unrelenting focus on collaboration and support among all women. As Christie Nolan noted, "if we plan to change longstanding patterns in our society around power, then we should shine a light on it and make *intentional choices* to practicing a new form of power—*power that is collective,* so we all have ownership in the results." Finally, she proclaimed, "if we are ever are going to make a change, we have to unpack and understand it all. We then use the information to make conscious choices about how we lead going forward. We are going to be more inclusive. We are going to create a more equitable society, organization, or board of directors, or whatever is right in front of us, with the *intentional and deliberate* choices that we make."

On Character as a Required Foundational Trait

There was great consensus among the women leaders on the key importance of *Character* as an essential requirement for exercising power and sustaining its staying power. Self-knowledge, the selfless goals of exercising power to benefit others and pursuing the truth at all times resonated with all the subjects. They all expressed strong and bold personal commitments to these values and personal traits. For example, Rosemarie explained that "it would be impossible to give anyone what you do not own or teach knowledge that you do not possess. If you want your team to have a clear sense of *right and wrong,* then you, as the leader, should not only know the difference by heart, but also live it accordingly. *Integrity, honesty, and sincerity* will allow you to consistently demonstrate that 'right is right' and 'wrong is wrong' by example."

Christie Nolan advised us to not only pursue the truth but to publicly speak the truth. She pointed out that "in meetings, I see a lot of women unable to have a voice, or not have enough courage to *speak their truth* for fear of being wrong, judged, or offending someone. I noticed this quite a bit, and I call it *polite dysfunction.* Women don't have the opportunity to get a word in because older men have the tendency to dominate the conversation. Women may not be as assertive because of the way we were raised, and others may consider it disrespectful to interrupt."

This statement from Christie is at the heart of the Character component of the WomenPower Paradigm. Implicit in pursuing the *Truth* is the courage to speak up and stand up for your cherished values, principles, and self-worth. Finding your *voice* and speaking the *Truth* entail knowing who you are and your personal value system. For example, if you value social justice and equality, you have to speak up and act to defend and to advocate for these principles. It's important to know when to speak up and when to simply listen. You might refrain from speaking up on every little issue that you disagree with, and also withhold judgment and speaking up until you have formed an informed stance on the subject. You also have to find your unique *voice*; you can't be an echo of someone else. Finding your voice can be a complex and challenging minuet, but it is a critical skill for leaders that can be learned with practice and determination. It gets easier the more you apply the skills and learn more about effective ways of communicating.

Secretary Jennifer Cohan's mission of *serving others*—working to motivate and empower employees, focusing on customer needs and requirements, leading a department to improve transportation safety, and commitment to community service—all point to a strength of character that's a categorical imperative for gaining and keeping power. Her lofty goal of promoting the *common good* is powered by her limitless and desirable *personal traits,* such as hard work, determination, infectious optimism, courage, and a sense of gratitude for her mentors and followers.

On the Eight Core Competencies of Powerful Women

The chorus of voices in the preceding chapters clearly affirms the integrity and usefulness of the eight competencies listed in the WomenPower Paradigm, with the exception of Congresswoman Blunt Rochester's recommendation on adding *lifelong learning.*

Another female leader, Christie Nolan, echoed the congresswoman's sentiments concerning the fundamental value of lifelong learning. Christie noted, "as a lifelong learner, I have always read books to evolve and grow. But I also do self-work to look at patterns of behavior in my life. Then I begin to understand my insecurities and my blind spots. Now I read to even be more helpful to others in their work on themselves. As a leader, I'm always asking the question, whether to an individual or organization, what they need, and how I can add value to them. I listen."

Christie is on target. Active listening to what others are saying is critical to learning and growing. It's nearly impossible to learn and change ineffective behaviors, if you don't listen to feedback from other individuals. Active listening is a prerequisite for gaining effective communication skills, one of the eight competencies in the WomenPower Paradigm.

Leadership and Management: Here are some comments from our subjects on the relevance of leadership and management as key competencies to develop and nurture. Rosemarie, one of our remarkable leaders, stated "being a leader is first of all showing a good example to your followers. If followers cannot find anything worth emulating from you, you have failed as a leader. Because leadership is influencing people to do what you want them to, not by force or out of fear, the key is getting them to cooperate without much effort on your side. For that, followers have to believe that you are leading them to the right goal or the one you set with them."

Communication Skills: In terms of *communication skills*, Beth-Ann felt that listening without judging, communicating precisely and clearly, and avoiding "vagueness" are fundamental to effective communication. Secretary Jennifer Cohan's employees are amazed at her ability to communicate effectively with all types of people, and her success in navigating the treacherous waters of the political environment. Not only is she able to communicate her vision to the funding agency, she is also knowledgeable in the budget process and has incrementally built powerful connections with decision makers.

People Skills: Our in-house organizational development expert,

Christie Nolan, recalled how "I developed the ability to quickly *read people and situations* at a very young age. I also had a sense or strong moral compass of what is right and wrong early on. Both are keys to *people skills.* I believe that gaining power is all about *relationship building*, because we can't really achieve or do anything without others. We all want to be part of something that is bigger than any one of us can do alone. We connect with people, build bridges, and nurture relationships, because it is in partnership that we are able to create change."

According to Rosemarie, developing *people skills* is crucial to leadership. She said that it is critical to remember that co-workers are people; they are not inanimate objects or robots that will move, respond, talk, or follow commands at the push of a button. "You should know how to handle people with emotional intelligence," Rosemarie remarked. She underscores the importance of people skills by linking it to the very essence of power. She defines power as the ability to accomplish goals through *people.* "Power lies in influencing people to do what you want them to do to reach your common goals," she explained.

Emotional Intelligence: Christie proclaimed that "Emotional Intelligence (EQ) is the foundation for everything, including power. In order to be powerful, one needs to have a high level of EQ. I break down EQ into: (1) self-awareness and self-management, (2) relationship awareness and relationship management. The ability to reflect on who we are, being self-aware or understanding of others' perception of us—be it as woman, minority, or somebody young—can be a valuable competency to have when discerning how to approach a situation."

Problem-Solving and Decision-Making Skills: Beth-Ann's direct reports and peers admire her for her ability to resolve conflict, where everyone is a winner. It's a competency that they appreciate and value in Beth-Ann. They applaud her ability to deal with difficult people and challenging situations by actively listening to both sides of the issue and by remaining fair and non-judgmental. Consequently, her employees feel heard and validated, and conflict is resolved to everyone's satisfaction. The Congresswoman also highlighted the importance of being able to solve problems and make decisions as skills that women need to nurture and develop. She pointed out that women need to be decisive, even when people make you question your decisions. She stressed that there's a need "to be decisive, since you can't make everybody happy."

Political Skills: Beth-Ann affirmed the critical importance of political skill at every level of any organization, as well as building strong and resilient relationships and a deep understanding of the power structure within a system. Congresswoman Lisa Blunt Rochester also noted the importance of possessing political skills. She pointed out that "politics is not a bad word." We need to be politically savvy to "navigate strategically and to be able to communicate the message effectively."

Subject Matter Expertise: Great leaders are great teachers and mentors. Jennifer Cohan is also an adjunct instructor at Wilmington University, in addition to her full-time position as a top-level cabinet secretary. She is captivated and inspired by her students when the fabled "Aha!" moment happens. There was great consensus among the employees I interviewed that Jennifer is a great and outstanding leader because of her focus on customers and employees; her exceptional ability to communicate effectively and listen actively to the voices of customers; her use of data when making informed and quick decisions; and her *subject matter expertise.*

As was noted before, these competencies are situational and are amenable to change depending on such factors as changing political, economic, social, and technological environments. They vary depending on the context—factors such as employees' needs and requirements, customer preferences, tasks and timelines, and other situational variables need to be considered.

Path Forward

Our vision is to improve the abilities of women and girls to gain and sustain power, to be comfortable wielding it so that it becomes a natural and reflexive posture that is part of their behavioral repertoire. Our mission also involves the liberation of both women and men's attitudes towards cultural roles, gender domination, and equality and freedom of choice in roles and relationships. It's our intention to support all genders in embracing the value of mutual respect, personal and professional growth, and self-actualization. Here are some of the initial steps that we intend to implement to start this initiative:

- **Women and Power and Executive Coaching:** Collaborate with the leaders and staff of the Office of Women's Advancement and Advocacy in training a cadre of executive mentors and coaches in developing the skills and competencies of women leaders in Delaware, using the WomenPower Paradigm as a framework.
- **Professional Development and Training in the Workplace:** Design a Women and Power Curriculum, using the WomenPower Paradigm as a core component. Partner with the trainers and educators of the Delaware Department of Human Resources, Delaware State University, Wilmington University, and the University of Delaware in designing a model curriculum. The training could be offered as a daylong seminar, a two to three-day workshop, a certificate program, or a university course. Instructional methods could include interactive lectures, panel discussions, case studies, collaborative learning, small group discussions, simulations, practicum, internships, and other hands-on and experiential modalities.
- **Fund for Women:** Expand the existing Delaware Fund for Women to include stipends and scholarships to support the continuing education and training of women in the area of women and power.

Parting Words: "To live past the end of your myth...."

When I was working as deputy director for a large department of the State of Delaware, I decided to retire early, because I was searching for larger meaning and purpose and I wanted to be certain that I didn't "overstay my welcome." My intent was to leave state employment while people still valued my abilities and contributions to the organization. It was the best decision I ever made—it not only benefited the organization but this early exit also promoted my personal and professional growth. As Canadian poet Anne Carson warned us, "to live past the end of your myth is a perilous thing." There are instances when political leaders, business leaders, CEOs, and other powerful figures "overstay their welcome" and fail to see the warning signs: the waning powers of their intellect, the misalignment between their skills and the organizational imperatives, and the needs and requirements of their customers and stakeholders, and other telltale signs of leadership degradation and decay. Still, they persist, and they resist.

The temporal nature and sacredness of power dictate that we relinquish it when "we're the wrong man or woman for the wrong time" or when the greater good demands a new face and a new power model. We are called upon to move on, find our true north, rather than holding on to a tenuous state of inelegant decay. The brutal irony of this intransigent state is that we're the last ones to know when it's time to leave. Although, if we pause and try to listen to the whisper of that little voice within us, quietly screaming, "it's time to exit!" we might just overcome the inertia of fear and failure. Let's have the courage and the audacity to reflect and to move on, leave a lasting legacy, and transfer power to the next generation of trailblazers and leaders.

Appendix:
Women and Power Study
Questionnaires

QUESTIONNAIRE 1
Del Tufo Consulting, LLC—"Empowering Minds"
Female Leaders–December 2018

Your insights and feedback are critical in helping us improve the professional and personal skills and abilities of women to effectively achieve and keep power and influence. As a result of this effort, we hope to offer women evidence-based guidelines for action that have the potential of improving women's abilities to achieve and keep their version of power and influence.

Instructions: Based on your positive experience as a *successful woman leader*, please respond to the following questions. Place a check mark right beside the response/responses that apply and explain your answers in the comment sections.

1. Background information: Tell me about yourself and your career (early life, career and journey to the present time).

_____
_____
_____
_____
_____
_____
_____

2. **The WHO: Who inspired and influenced you to be the powerful woman that you are today?**

_____

_____

_____

_____

_____

_____

_____

_____

_____

_____

_____

_____

_____

_____

3. **CHARACTER: What qualities and traits should women adopt to be able to gain and keep power?**

- Self-knowledge
- Exercise power in service of others
- Exercise power for the common good
- Practice universally-accepted desirable **values,** such as honesty, integrity, courage, and the like
- Relentless pursuit of the truth
- All of the above
- Others

COMMENTS: Please explain your response.

_____

_____

_____

_____

_____

_____

_____

_____

_____

_____

_____

_____

4. EIGHT COMPETENCIES: What professional competencies should women adopt and master to be able to gain and keep power?

- Management and leadership
- Communication skills
- People skills
- Emotional intelligence
- Problem solving and decision-making skills
- Conflict resolution skills
- Political skills
- Subject matter expertise or be competent in some specific area
- All of the above
- Others

COMMENTS: Please explain your response.

_____

_____

_____

_____

_____

_____

_____

_____

_____

_____

_____

_____

_____

_____

_____

5. How can we best assist women in their struggle to achieve parity in power and influence?

_____

_____

_____

_____

_____

_____

_____

_____

_____

_____

_____

6. What attitudes or behaviors should women change?

_____

_____

_____

_____

_____

_____

_____

_____

_____

_____

_____

7. OTHER RECOMMENDATIONS FOR IMPROVEMENT: Do you have any other suggestions on how women can gain and keep power effectively?

Women and Power Study Questionnaires

_____
_____
_____
_____
_____
_____
_____
_____
_____
_____
_____
_____
_____
_____
_____
_____
_____

8. Is there anything else that you would like to tell us that we have not asked?

_____
_____
_____
_____
_____
_____
_____
_____

9. Do you have any other comments or questions?

_____
_____
_____
_____
_____
_____
_____
_____

QUESTIONNAIRE 2
Del Tufo Consulting, LLC—"Empowering Minds"
Male Respondents: December 2018

Your insights and feedback are critical in helping us improve the professional and personal skills and abilities of women to effectively achieve and keep power and influence. As a result of this effort, we hope to offer women an evidence-based guideline for action that has the potential of improving women's abilities to achieve and keep their version of power and influence.

Instructions: Based on your positive experience with a *woman leader,* please respond to the following questions. Place a check mark right beside the response/responses that apply and explain your answers in the comment sections.

1. CHARACTER: What qualities and traits should women adopt to be able to gain and keep power?

- Self-knowledge
- Exercise power in service of others
- Exercise power for the common good
- Practice universally-accepted desirable **values,** such as honesty, integrity, courage, and the like
- Relentless pursuit of the truth
- Personal traits, such as self-confidence, flexibility, optimism, tenacity, to name a few
- All of the above
- Others

COMMENTS: Please explain your response.

_____

_____

_____

_____

_____

_____

_____

_____
_____
_____
_____
_____
_____
_____

2. EIGHT COMPETENCIES: What professional competencies should women adopt and master to be able to gain and keep power?

- Management and leadership
- Communication skills
- People skills
- Emotional intelligence
- Problem solving and decision-making skills
- Conflict resolution skills
- Political skills
- Subject matter expertise or be competent in some specific area
- All of the above
- Others

COMMENTS: Please explain your response.

_____
_____
_____
_____
_____
_____

3. What attitudes or behaviors should they change?

_____
_____
_____

_____
_____
_____
_____
_____
_____
_____
_____
_____
_____
_____

4. OTHER RECOMMENDATIONS FOR IMPROVE-MENT: Do you have any other suggestions on how women can gain and keep power effectively?

_____
_____
_____
_____
_____
_____
_____

5. Is there anything else that you would like to tell us that we have not asked?

_____
_____
_____
_____
_____
_____

6. Do you have any other comments or questions?

_____
_____
_____
_____

QUESTIONNAIRE 3
Women and Power Study
Del Tufo Consulting, LLC—"Empowering Minds"
Employee/Peer Assessment Survey: December 2018

Your insights and feedback are critical in helping us improve the professional and personal skills and abilities of women to effectively achieve and keep power and influence. As a result of this effort, we hope to offer women an evidence-based guideline for action that has the potential of improving women's abilities to achieve and keep their version of power and influence.

Instructions: Based on your positive experience with a *woman leader,* please respond to the following questions.

    1. **Tell us about your leader/peer's leadership skills and ability to handle power (Influence-potential).**

_____
_____
_____
_____
_____
_____
_____
_____
_____
_____
_____
_____
_____
_____
_____

    2. **List and discuss 3–5 areas of leadership and power that your leader/peer excels in.**

_____
_____
_____

_____
_____
_____
_____
_____
_____
_____
_____
_____
_____
_____
_____

3. What attitudes or behaviors should she change/modify to be a more effective leader?

_____
_____
_____
_____
_____
_____
_____
_____
_____
_____
_____
_____
_____
_____

4. Other Recommendations for Improvement: Do you have any other suggestions on how *women in general* can gain and keep power effectively?

_____
_____
_____

_____
_____
_____
_____
_____
_____
_____
_____
_____
_____
_____

References

Aitken, Jonathan. (2013). *Margaret Thatcher: Power and personality*. New York, New York: Bloomsbury.

Allison, S. T., & Goethals, G. R. (2014). "Now he belongs to the ages: The heroic leadership dynamic and deep narratives of greatness." In G.R. Goethals, et al. (Eds.), *Conceptions of leadership: Enduring ideas and emerging insights*. (pp. 167–184). New York, New York: Palgrave Macmillan.

American Institute of Physics. *Marie Curie and the Science of Radioactivity*. (2000). https://history.aip.org/exhibits/curie/recdis2.htm.

American Society for Quality. "Value stream mapping tutorial-What is VSM?" asq. org/quality-resources/lean/value-stream-mapping.

Bacharach, Samuel, B. (2005). *Get them on your side: Win support, convert skeptics, get results*. Avon, Massachusetts: Adams Media Corporation.

Beard, Mary. (2017). *Women & power: A manifesto*. New York, New York: Liveright Publishing Corporation.

Biography.com. Editors. (2014, April 2, updated 2019, June 23). *Rosalind Franklin biography, chemist, scientist (1920–1958)*. https://www.biography.com/scientist/rosalind-franklin.

Blumburg, Naomi. "*Yousafzai, Malala*." In *Britanica*. https://www.britannica.com/biography/Malala-Yousafzai.

Breyer, Melissa. (2013, March 28). *Ten accidental inventions that changed the world*. www.mnn.com/leaderboard/stories/10-accidental-inventions-that-changed-the-world.

Breyer, Melissa. (2017, June 5). *Ten Accidental Inventions that Changed the World*. www.mnn.com/leaderboard/stories/10-accidental-inventions-that-changed-the-world.

Brown, Brené (2018). *Dare to lead. Brave work. Tough conversations. Whole hearts*. New York, New York: Random House.

Broyles, Addle. (2011, July 18). *Guest post: A Sociological study: Why so few women chefs in restaurant kitchens*. The Feminist Kitchen Website. https://thefeministkitchen.com/2011/07/18/guest-post-a-sociological-study-of-why-so-few-women-chefs-in-restaurant-kitchens/.

Business Insider (2011, February 20). *The 15 most powerful members of skull and bones*. Retrieved December 23, 2018 from www.businessinsider.com/skull-and-bones-alumni-2011-2.

Center for American Progress. *The women's leadership gap*. https://www.americanprogress.org/issues/women/reports/2018/11/20/461273/womens-leadership-gap-2/.

Chefs and Head Cooks. (2019). *Data USA website*. Retrieved from https://datausa.io/profile/soc/chefs-head-cooks.

References

CNN. *Are you an old millennial or a young millennial?* www.cnn.com/2017/05/01/health/young-old-millennial-partner/index.html.

Coelho, Paulo. (1988). *The alchemist.* New York, New York: HarperCollins Publishers.

Covey, Stephen, M.R. (2006). *The speed of trust: The one thing that changes everything.* New York, New York: The Free Press.

Crossman, Ashley. *Definition of power structure.* Retrieved from www.sociology.about.com/od/P_Index/g/Power-Structure.

Dalailama.com. *Birth to Exile: The 14th Dalai Lama.* www.dalailama.com/the-dalai-lama/biography-and-daily-life/birth-to-exile.

Davies, Rhodri. (2016). *Myanmar is most generous nation - 2016 World giving index. Charities Aid Foundation.* www.cafonline.org/about-us/blog-home/giving-thought/how-giving-works/2016.

Delaware Libraries *What's your passion?* (2018). https://whatsyourpassion.lib.de.us/jennifer-cohan/.

Del Tufo, Theresa. (2015). *The fullness of nothing: Discover the hidden joy that surrounds you.* Melbourne, Florida: Motivational Press.

Dillard, Sarah, & Lipschitz, Vanessa. (2014, November 6). *Research: How female CEOs actually get to the top.* Harvard Business Review. https://hbr.org/2014/11/research-how-female-ceos-actually-get-to-the-top.

Domhoff, G. William. (2005). *Who rules America? Power, politics and social change.* New York, New York: McGraw-Hill.

Elliott, Ellen (2016, July). *Women in science: Remembering Rosalind Franklin.* Blog Post, The Jackson Laboratory. https://www.jax.org/news-and-insights/jax-blog/2016/july/women-in-science-rosalind-franklin.

Fieldstad, Elisha. (2019, March 26). *Virginia's first black female police chief says she was forced to resign.* https://www.nbcnews.com/news/us-news/virginia-s-first-black-female-police-chief-says-she-was-n987501.

Friedan, Betty. (1963). *The Feminine mystique.* New York, New York: W.W. Norton & Company.

Fry, Richard. (2018). *Millennials are the largest generation in the U.S. labor force. Pew Research Center.* www.pewresearch.org/fact-tank/2018/04/11/millennials-largest-generation-us.

Gallup Study. 2015. *State of the American manager: Analytic and advice for leaders.* Retrieved from www.gallup.com/services/182138/state-american-manager.aspx.

Garber, Peter, R. (2008). *50 Communications activities, icebreakers and exercises.* Amherst, Mass. HRD Press, Inc.

Giles, Sunnie. (2016, March 15). *The most important leadership competencies, according to world leaders.* https://hbr.org/2016/03/the-most-important-leadership-competencies-according-to-leaders-around-the-world.

Goleman, Daniel. (2013, December). *The Focused leader.* www.hbr.org/2013/12/the-focused-leader.

Goodall, Jane. (2018, March 9). *Dr. Jane Goodall: Being a woman was crucial to my success in a male-dominated field.* https://time.com/5192249/jane-goodall-sexism-gender-equality-documentary/.

Greene, Robert. (2000). *The 48 laws of power.* New York, New York: Penguin Book.

Greenhill, Sam (2008). *The royal apprentice: Prince William's two-year training programme on how to be king. The Daily Mail.* Retrieved from www.dailymail.co.uk/news/article-1038961/The-Royal-Apprentice-Prince-Williams.

Greenleaf Center for Servant Leadership. *What is servant leadership?* www.greenleaf.org/what-is-servant-leadership.

References

Greguletz, Elena; Diehl, Riitta-Marjo; & Kreutzer, Karin. (2018). "Why women build less effective networks than men: The role of structural exclusion and personal hesitation." *Journal of Human Relations*, 7(72), 1234-1261. https://doi.org/10.1177/0018726718804303.

Hammond, Michelle McKinney. (2014). *The Power of being a woman: Secrets to getting the life you want and the love you need.* Irvine, CA: Harvest House Publishers.

"Harrington, Penny." (2019). In *Wikipedia, the Free Encyclopedia Website.* https://en.wikipedia.org/wiki/Penny_Harrington.

"Harvard, Beverly, 1950." (2019, September 30). *Encyclopedia Website.* https://www.encyclopedia.com/education/news-wires-white-papers-and-books/harvard-beverly-1950.

Heilbrun, Carolyn, G. (1988). *Writing a woman's life.* New York, New York: Ballantine Books.

Howe, Neil & Strauss, William. (2000). *Millennials rising: The next generation.* New York, New York: Vintage Books.

Hunter, Floyd. (1963). *Community power structure: A study of decision makers.* New York, New York: Anchor Books.

Kaiser, Robert B. & Kaplan, Robert E. (2013). "Thatcher's Greatest Strength Was Her Greatest Weakness." Harvard Business Review. https://hbr.org/2013/04/thatchers-greatest-strength-was.

Keith, Phil. (2019, March). *Director's corner: Women in policing.* COPS Office Website. https://cops.usdoj.gov/html/dispatch/03-2019/directors_message.html.

Keltner, Dacher. (2017). *The Power paradox: How we gain and lose influence.* New York, New York: Penguin Books.

Kolditz, Thomas. (2007). *In Extremis leadership: Leading as if your life depended on it.* Hoboken, New Jersey: Jossey-Bass.

Koren, Leonard. (1994). *Wabi-sabi for artists, designers, poets and philosophers.* Southbridge, Massachusetts: Stonebridge Press.

Labor Force Statistics from the Current Population Survey. (2019, January 18). Bureau of Labor Statistics, United States Department of Labor Website. https://www.bls.gov/cps/cpsaat39.htm.

Lawrence, Robyn Griggs (2001, September-October). *Wabi-sabi: The Art of imperfection. Utne Reader.* http://www.utne.com/mind-and-body/wabi-sabi.aspx.

Lemlij, Moises & Milones, Luis. (2017). *Women: power & prestige in Andean Society.* Yolanda Carlessi Publisher.

Lipman, George. (2015, April 23). *Are women better than men?* www.forbes.com/sites/victorlipman/2015/04/16/are-women-really-as-this-major.

Maddox, Brenda. (2001). *Rosalind Franklin: The dark lady of DNA.* New York, New York: HarperCollins.

Marcal, Katherine. (2016). *Who cooked Adam Smith's dinner?* New York, NY: Pegasus Books Ltd.

Marie Curie Care and Support through Terminal Illness. (2019). *Marie Curie the scientist.* (2019). Retrieved August 1, 2019 from https://www.mariecurie.org.uk/who/our-history/marie-curie-the-scientist.

MCenery, Thornton. (2011). *The 15 Most Influential members of skull and bones.* Business Insider. Retrieved from www.businessinsider.com.au/skull-and-bones-alumni-2011-2.

McKeeman, Sam. (2012). *Curriculum on Ethics.* Unpublished.

McKinsey and Company Study. (2016, February 1). McKinsey Quarterly. https://

References

www.mckinsey.com/business-functions/organization/our-insights/millennials-burden-blessing-or-both#.

McSpadden, Kevin (2015, May 14). *You now have a shorter attention span than a goldfish*. Retrieved from www.time.com/3858309/attention-spans-goldfish.

Morgan, Howard. (2005). *The Art and practice of leadership coaching*. Somerset, New Jersey: Wiley Publishers.

Moulton, John Fletcher. (1924). *Obedience to the unenforceable*. The Atlantic Monthly. Retrieved www.thegathering.com/obedience-to-the-unenforceable.

Muench, U., Sindelar, J., Busch, S., & Buerhaus, P. (2015, March 24/31). *Salary differences between male and female registered nurses in the United States*. JAMA Website. Retrieved from https://jamanetwork.com/journals/jama/fullarticle/2208795.

Muller, Wayne. (1996). *How then shall we live*. New York, New York: Bantam Books.

Nagengast, Larry. (2017, June 4). *Lisa Blunt Rochester is ready to shake things up*. Delaware Today. Retrieved from www.delawaretoday.com/Delaware-Today/June-2017/Lisa-Blunt-Rochester-is-Ready-to-Shake-Things-Up.

National Nurses Day/ National Nurses Week. (2017, May 6). United States Census Website. Retrieved from https://www.census.gov/newsroom/stories/2017/may/cb17-sfs42-nurses.html.

Northouse, P. G. (2016). *Leadership: Theory and practice* (7th ed.). Los Angeles, California: SAGE Publications Ltd.

O'Neill, Mary Beth. (2000). *Executive coaching: with backbone and heart*. San Francisco, CA: Jossey-Bass: A Wiley Company.

Perrewe, Pamela. (2006). *Want to get ahead at work? Hone your political skills*. www.fsu.edu/news/2006/04/26/political.skills.

Pew Research Center. (2016, May). *Survey of law enforcement officers*. www.assets.pewresearch.org/wp content/uploads/sites/3/2017/01/06171402/Police-Report_FINAL.

Pew Research Center. (2017). *Women in majority-male workplaces*. www.pewresearch.org/fact-tank/2018/03/07/women-in-majority-male-workplaces.

Pew Research Center. (2017, May). *Trends and patterns in intermarriage*. www.pewsocialtrends.org/2017/05/18/1-trends-and-patterns-in-intermarriage.

Pew Research Center Analysis of Census Data. (2017). Retrieved on November 12, 2018 from https://pewrsr.ch/2uVqhbs.

Rabasca Roepe, Lisa. (2018, December 17). *The Hidden networking gap between men and women*. https://www.fastcompany.com/90277129/the-hidden-networking-gap-between-men-and-women.

Salovey, Peter & Mayer, John. (1990). "Imagination, cognition, and personality." In *Emotional intelligence* 9, 185–211. DOI: https://doi.org/10.2190/DUGG-P24E-52WK-6CDG.

Sayre, Anne. (1975). *Rosalind Franklin and DNA*. New York, NewYork: W.W. Norton & Company.

Scarborough, William. (2018). *What the data says about women in management between 1980 and 2010*. Harvard Business Review. hbr.org/2018/02/what-the-data-says-about-women-in-management-between-1980-and-2010.

Statista. (2017, July). *Women—Statistics and facts*. www.statista.com/topics/1269/women.

Stevenson, Jane E. & Orr, Evelyn. (2017). *We interviewed 57 female CEOs to find out how more women can get to the top*. Harvard Business Review. https://hbr.org/2017/11/we-interviewed-57-female-ceos-to-find-out-how-more-women-can-get-to-the-top.

References

Tecco, Halle. (2017). *Women in health Care 2017: How does our industry stack up?* Rock Health https://rockhealth.com/reports/women-in-healthcare-2017-how-does-our-industry-stack-up/.

Thatcher, Margaret. (1995). *The Path to power.* London, England: HarperCollins UK.

Thio, Alex. (1992). *Sociology: An introduction.* New York, New York: HarperCollins Publishers, Inc.

Thompson, G., & Vecchio, R. P. (2009). *Situational leadership theory: A test of three versions. The Leadership Quarterly,* 20(5), 837–848. DOI: http://dx.doi.org.ezaccess.libraries.psu.edu/10.1016/j.leaqua.2009.06.014.

Trapani, Gina & Jacobs, Matt. (2019). *Narrow the gap website.* Retrieved September 18, 2019 from https://narrowthegap.co/gap/chefs-and-head-cooks.

Twenge, Jean. (2014). *Generation me: Why today's young Americans are more confident, assertive, entitled—and more miserable than ever before.* New York, New York: Atria Press.

U.S. Census Bureau. (2010). *The Delaware Census State Data Center. Archived from the original on December 31, 2016.* www.census.gov/quickfacts/DE.

U.S. Census Bureau. (2011). *Percentage of nurses who are men from 1970 to 2011.* https://www.census.gov/content/dam/Census/newsroom/releases/2013/cb13-32_figure1-hi.jpg.

U.S. Census Bureau. (2013). *Male nurses becoming more commonplace.* https://www.census.gov/newsroom/press-releases/2013/cb13-32.html.

U.S. Census Bureau. (2013) *Men in nursing occupations.* www.census.gov/.../blogs/random-samplings/2013/02/men-in-nursing-occupations.html.

U.S. Census Bureau. *The Changing economics and demographics of young adulthood: 1975–2016.* Retrieved on January 2, 2019 from www.census.gov/library/publications/2017/demo/p20-579.html.

"United States presidential approval rating." In Wikipedia. www. https://en.wikipedia.org/wiki/United_States_presidential_approval_rating.

Van Tongeren, D. R., Green, J. D., Davis, D. E., Hook, J. N., & Hulsey, T. L. (2016). "Prosociality enhances meaning in life." *The Journal of Positive Psychology,* 11(3), 225–236. http://www.tandfonline.com/doi/abs/10.1080/17439760.2015.1048814?journalCode=rpos20&)=&.

Vejnoska, Jill. (2016). *Top cop Beverly Harvard broke down many doors.* The Atlanta Journal-Constitution. https://www.ajc.com/lifestyles/top-cop-beverly-harvard-broke-down-many-doors/IELgxkHkrwUIo9F6i4qR6L/.

Velasquez, M., Andre, C., Shanks, T., & Meyer, M. (2010). *What is ethics?* Markkula Center for Applied Ethics. www.scu.edu/ethics/ethics-resources/ethical-decision-making/what-is-ethics.

Wallis, Jim. (2013). *Whatever happened to the "common good"?* www.ideas.time.com/2013/04/04/whatever-happened-to-the-common-good.

Warden, C. *Positive political skills.* Retrieved from www.cwarden.org/warden/downloads/busPsyc/Ch11.pdf.

Warner, J., Ellmann, N., & Boesch, D. (2018). *The women's leadership gap.* Center for American Progress. www.americanprogress.org/.../reports/2018/11/20/461273/womens-leadership-gap-2.

Watson, James D. (1968). *The Double helix: A personal account of the discovery of the structure of the DNA.* New York, New York: Touchstone of Simon & Schuster, Inc.

Why are there so few female chefs—the gender balance in the culinary industry. (2019). Chefify. https://www.chefify.net/academy/article/why-are-there-so-few-female-chefs-gender-balance-culinary-industry.

References

WMFC.Org. *Generational Differences Chart.* (2019). http://www.wmfc.org/uploads/GenerationalDifferencesChartUpdated2019.pdf.

Yousafzai, Malala Biography. www.biography.com/.amp/people/malala-yousafzai-21362253.

Yousafzai, Malala. Yousafzai, Malala turns 20: Facts on her extraordinary life. https://www.biography.com/news/malala-yousafzai-facts-20th-birthday.

Zacharek, Stephanie. *Three queens to rule them all.* http://time.com/5466482/the-favourite-mary-queen-of-scots/.

Zheng, W., Kark, R., & Meister, A. (2018). *How women manage the gendered norms of leadership.* Harvard Business Review. https://hbr.org/2018/11/how-women-manage-the-gendered-norms-of-leadership.

Zigarmi, P., & Hoekstra, J. (2010). "Strategies for Leading a Change." In K. Blanchard (Ed.), *Leading at a higher Level.* (pp. 215-240). Upper Saddle River, New Jersey: Blanchard Management Corporation.

Zoom, Doktor. (2019). *Elizabeth Warren sending her aunt Bee to give everybody childcare!* Wonkette. https://www.wonkette.com/elizabeth-warren-sending-her-aunt-bee-to-give-everybody-childcare.

Index

Index